THE STAMP OF FDR

New Deal Post Offices in the Mid-Hudson Valley

BERNICE L. THOMAS

PURPLE MOUNTAIN PRESS • FLEISCHMANNS, NEW YORK

THE STAMP OF FDR
New Deal Post Offices in the Mid-Hudson Valley

First Edition 2002

Published by
Purple Mountain Press, Ltd.
1060 Main Street, P.O. Box 309, Fleischmanns, New York 12430
845-254-4062, 845-254-4476 (fax), purple@catskill.net
http://www.catskill.net/purple

Printing of the color plates in this book was made possible by a grant from Furthermore, the publication program of the J. M. Kaplan Fund.

Library of Congress Control Number: 2002106397
Manufactured in the United States of America
Printed on acid-free paper   1 2 3 4 5

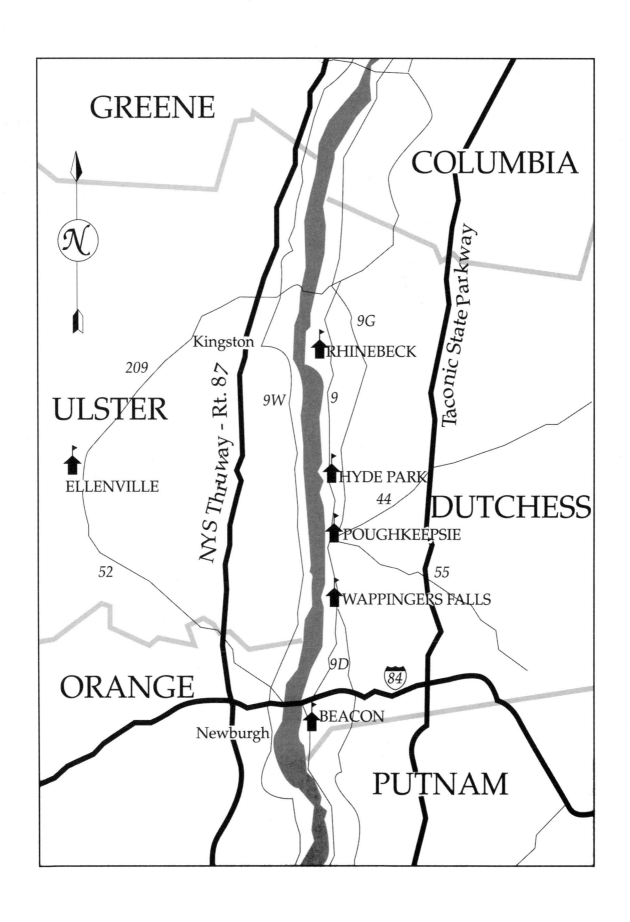

1882
1982

USA
20c

Franklin D. Roosevelt

CONTENTS

THE STAMP OF FDR

Introduction

SIX FEDERAL POST OFFICES in the Mid-Hudson Valley stand out as a group from the eleven hundred post offices built throughout America during the Great Depression. The distinctive Dutch Colonial revival buildings with murals on the lobby walls—five in towns strung like a necklace along the eastern shore of the Hudson River and a sixth across the river in Ellenville—all bear what the *Ellenville Journal* called "FDR's Stamp."[1] How and why these buildings bear the special imprint of the president of the United States makes for a fascinating story.

President Roosevelt determined the unique Dutch Colonial architectural style of the post offices in Beacon, Wappingers Falls, Poughkeepsie, Hyde Park, Rhinebeck, and Ellenville, asking that a historic building in each locale be used as a model. The building material had to be fieldstone, salvaged from the area wherever possible. The stone should be laid up in a simple vernacular format. The murals in the lobbies received the same meticulous attention. The president helped select the subject matter, reviewed the artists's sketches as the work progressed, and made corrections as he saw fit. Today the art and architecture of these New Deal post offices, standing in all but one instance in his home territory of Dutchess County, serve as a highly personal testimonial to Franklin Delano Roosevelt, revealing his interests, his beliefs, and his political accomplishments.

"Franklin D. Roosevelt, Architect"

FDR's inordinate concern with this group of fieldstone post offices indicates one thing first and foremost: a serious commitment to architecture and design. Indeed, Roosevelt sometimes thought of himself as an architect. He likened himself on one occasion to Thomas Jefferson, architect of Monticello, although he probably knew he lacked this president's architectural inventiveness.[2] A young Georgia

OPPOSITE

TOP: Cornerstone of the Poughkeepsie post office.

BOTTOM: James Roosevelt Memorial Library.

architect, Henry J. Toombs, designed a number of buildings for FDR, beginning with Eleanor Roosevelt's Hyde Park retreat, Val-Kill cottage, in 1925. Toombs also designed the James Roosevelt Memorial Library for Roosevelt's mother the following year. Franklin Roosevelt always had a commanding hand in the outcome. When the time came for Toombs to design a comparable retreat for the president in 1938, partly out of pique for so much interference by the president and partly for "fun," Toombs asked permission of the president to sign the drawings: "Franklin D. Roosevelt, Architect" and "Henry J. Toombs, Associate." Permission was granted. Roosevelt allowed the architect to publicize the signed drawings in *Life* magazine, which raised a furor in some quarters. Frank Lloyd Wright's architect son, John Lloyd Wright, wrote to *Life* to declare: "The moral breakdown and the integrity of the architectural profession now seems complete."[3]

Harlan Althen's article in the *New York Times Magazine* in 1940, "F. D. R. As Architect," was more appreciative of Roosevelt's architectural endeavors in the Mid-Hudson Valley.[4] The author understood that there was a purpose beyond the president's delight in the art of building. FDR believed in the necessity of preserving prerevolutionary Dutch Colonial houses in the Hudson River Valley. These houses made of stone strewn lavishly over the landscape by the Great Glacier were fast disappearing. One way Roosevelt chose to preserve them was through replication. The post offices replicating historic buildings and incorporating stones from early structures in the vicinity served the president's purpose especially well.

FDR as Dutchess County Historian

The history of Dutchess County, where his ancestral roots went back for generations, held a real fascination for FDR. He joined the Dutchess County Historical Society in Poughkeepsie in 1914, the year of its founding, serving as vice president for Hyde Park. FDR was town historian for Hyde Park between 1926 and 1931. In this capacity, he was responsible for the publication of the *Records of the Town of Hyde Park*. Roosevelt's penchant for preserving records of the past manifested itself during his presidential years in the formation of the National Archives and Records Service. FDR continued to involve himself in research and writing on local history, contributing articles on occasion to the Society's annual *Year Book*.[5] In another form of record keeping, he was the force behind the Holland Society's proposed two volume catalog of Dutch houses in the Hudson

Valley before 1776. He worked closely with the author of the volume pertaining to Dutchess County, Helen Wilkinson Reynolds, and contributed the introduction.[6] In the introduction, he tells of his distress when he discovered that houses he had seen as a boy were no longer extant. And often there were no photographs or drawings to help keep the memory alive. The photographs reproduced in Reynolds's volume were meant to document the houses before it was too late. FDR's consuming interest in Dutchess County history and its preservation, coupled with his zeal for architecture and design, goes a long way in explaining why this particular group of post offices took the form that they did.

FDR speaks to Dutchess County Historical Society at Springwood, Sept. 16, 1927.
(Franklin D. Roosevelt Library)

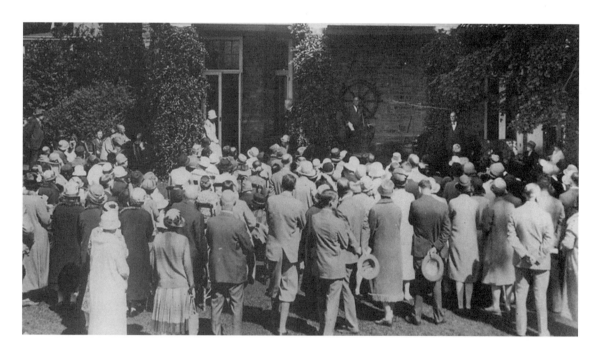

OPPOSITE

Beacon Post Office located at
369 Main Street.

THE STAMP OF FDR

Beacon:
Where It All Began

Franklin D. Roosevelt

FDR'S POLITICAL ASSOCIATIONS with Beacon go back to the beginning of his career. He gave his first election-eve speech in Beacon in 1910 when he ran for state senator, which launched a tradition there and in towns up and down the Hudson for the next thirty years. His informal remarks in 1940 noted that the day before election was his sixth visit to Beacon "to say howdy-do to a lot of my old neighbors."[7] Roosevelt began to write a column for the Beacon newspaper, the *Standard*, called "Between Neighbors" in August 1928. He gave up this outlet for his political opinions a few months later to devote more time to his campaign for governor of New York.[8]

Another tradition was launched in the 1910 campaign. Roosevelt decided to take the unprecedented step of campaigning in an automobile rather than in a horse drawn wagon. Both he and his advisors believed that this way, he would save much time, cover much more ground and be able to speak in many more communities.[9] No doubt the unusual sight of the candidate in a open red touring car, a Maxwell, helped the relatively unknown FDR win the election. An open touring car became a hallmark for him throughout his political lifetime.

The Beacon post office, dated 1936 on its cornerstone, was the first in the Mid-Hudson group. It did not actually open for business until October 1937. Like all New Deal post offices, the Beacon post office was authorized by the Procurement Division of the Treasury Department. The building cost $68,000, reflecting an allotment based on the amount of post office business. One percent of each allotment was reserved for interior decoration in the lobby. While the new federal post offices were intended to alleviate unemployment among American architects, they were not relief projects, in contrast to public programs like the Works Progress Administration (WPA). The Beacon archi-

FDR campaigning in Beacon's
Bank Square, November 1936.
(Beacon Historical Society)

tect Gilbert Stanley Underwood was one of twenty-one architects hired to work under Treasury's supervising architect Louis A. Simon to help cope with the expanding public building program of the Roosevelt New Deal.[10] Another incentive for the accelerated building program was Roosevelt's belief that government-sponsored architecture in America left much to be desired. He intended to add high-quality federal buildings to the American landscape during his tenure in office.

Secretary of the Treasury Henry J. Morgenthau Jr. explained the situation in his speech at the dedication of the Rhinebeck post office.[11] His department brought onto the staff in Washington twenty-one architects of recognized standing from different sections of the country, whose work was passed upon by four outstanding architects of national reputation. The aim was "not only to build buildings of maximum usefulness but to give them a character and a dignity that will be a genuine contribution to the advancement of architecture in the communities in which they have been built." All six post offices in the Mid-Hudson group were designed by one of the architects brought to Washington to fulfill the Treasury Department's mission. Secretary Morgenthau made a significant addition to his remarks in Rhinebeck: "In the ideas we have put into effect in the public building program we have followed the lead of one, whose enthusiastic interest in the project of building beautiful and serviceable and appropriate public buildings never flags." The person he was referring to was FDR.

THE STAMP OF FDR

Gilbert Stanley Underwood, Architect

Gilbert Stanley Underwood of Sun Valley, Idaho, worked extensively with the federal government under the public buildings programs of the 1930s, but the Beacon post office was his only federal building in New York State. He is noted for his work on the Los Angeles Federal Building, the U.S. Custom House in Seattle, Public Building Administration residence halls for women in Washington, D.C., and the San Francisco Mint.[12] This architect did his part in helping FDR achieve his goal of high-quality federal architecture.

The Beacon post office was not modeled after one particular historic building. It did, however, make a historic allusion. As the *Beacon News* noted: "The colonial stone building is in perfect sympathy with Beacon's outstanding Revolutionary history."[13] The building's fieldstone walls do conform to the group's set requirements. The stone was taken from the foundation of the old West Point Foundry in nearby Cold Spring. The architect actually rejected the stonework in its early stages in 1936, because "it is not satisfactory as a translation of the character of the design."[14] In the end, it did conform to a simple eighteenth-century look.

This modest, one-story Dutch Colonial revival building with its slate roof and attractive cupola topped by a weather vane has a decidedly federal cast, encouraged by a gabled pediment over the main section outlined in dentils and appliqued with a radiant golden eagle. The Poughkeepsie post office has a similarly disposed federal eagle, but it is not golden like the one in Beacon. It would not be surprising, all things considered, if the emblem did not have a special meaning for the president. Roosevelt was sworn in as a lifetime member of the Fraternal Order of Eagles in 1930 when he was governor of New York and presented with a solid gold membership card. He was following in the footsteps of his relative and hero, Theodore Roosevelt, who was also a lifetime member of the order. Both New York Roosevelts were commended in the organization's national newsletter in 1930 for their tenacious support of Old Age Pensions, something closely associated with the Fraternal Order of Eagles. In 1935, when the architecture of the Beacon post office was in the planning stage, Congress passed the Social Security Act with old age pensions a kingpin of the New Deal legislation. The unusual golden eagle on the Beacon facade might well be a sign, on one level, of a certain kind of political commitment.

Beacon's deceptively simple fieldstone exterior hides a

lobby rich in materials and decoration (Pls. Ia & b). Vermont marble in three shades of green covers the floor and a wainscotting six and a half feet high, above which are painted murals over all four walls and dividing arches at each end. A plaster cornice of triglyphs underlines the ceiling, and a row of florets defines the curve of each arch. A screen of bronze letter-boxes adds to the sumptuous effect of this interior.

Cornerstone of the Beacon Post Office, 1936, with inscription that begins: "Henry Morgenthau Jr Secretary of the Treasury."

FDR and Henry J. Morgenthau Jr., February 9, 1934. Photograph inscribed: "For Elinor [Morgenthau] from one of two of a kind Franklin D. Roosevelt."

(Franklin D. Roosevelt Library)

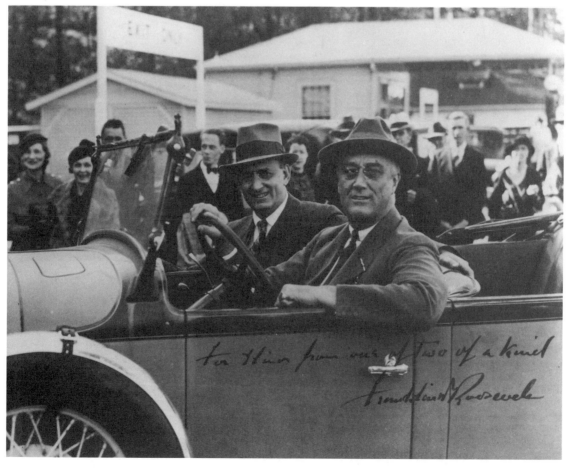

THE STAMP OF FDR

An Exceptional Cornerstone

The inscription on the Beacon cornerstone does not begin like the other five cornerstones in the group with "Franklin D. Roosevelt, President of the United States of America." Instead it begins, "Henry Morgenthau Jr., Secretary of the Treasury." No mention is made of the president. Although it is not labeled as such, the Beacon post office assuredly bears the stamp of FDR. When it is noted that "Morgenthau chose a stone building in the tradition of Dutchess County for Beacon," one can only believe that Secretary Morgenthau was doing President Roosevelt's bidding.[15] There are too many other correspondences between the Beacon post office and the rest of the group–such as reusing old stones from the area and mimicking early stone walls on the exterior--not to see the hand of FDR in this instance. Why the president's name and title does not lead the list of government dignitaries on the Beacon cornerstone is uncertain. Perhaps Roosevelt only decided to put his name on these Hudson Valley cornerstones by the time the next one was inscribed for Poughkeepsie in 1937. Perhaps allowing Morgenthau's name as secretary of the Treasury to head the list in Beacon was a matter of courtesy to his longtime friend and political ally, as well as the proper protocol for a building sponsored by the Treasury Department. And, as the newspaper observed when the post office opened, Beacon was Secretary Morgenthau's home town.

Murals by Charles Rosen

A distinguished member of the Woodstock, New York art colony, Charles Rosen executed the murals in 1937, assisted by Clarence Bolten. Rosen had headed the Art Students League of New York's Summer School of Landscape Painting in Woodstock from 1918 to 1922, after which he founded and headed the Woodstock School of Painting.[16] Rosen is representative of the high caliber of artists chosen to decorate the post offices in the Mid-Hudson group.

The choice of peach and aquamarine as the dominant colors give these attractive murals an unmistakable look of the 1930s. A sweeping forty foot by eighty foot pictorial map of the Hudson Valley divided into counties runs the full length of the room, with scenes of Beacon at each end. They include waterfalls, Mt. Beacon, churches, and a hat factory, plus city and county seals, and a map of the city (Pls. IIa & b). Among the little identifying images along the Hudson River is one labeled "Home of Franklin D. Roosevelt HYDE PARK." This appears on the wall directly

across from the entrance to the lobby, paired with an image of the "Vassar College Library POUGHKEEPSIE." Roosevelt became a trustee of Vassar College in 1923. One can trace FDR's ritualistic election-eve tour with stops on both sides of the Hudson River by following the trail of pictorial emblems on the map, including one labeled "Washington's Headquarters NEWBURGH." The tour always ended at "Springwood," his ancestral home in Hyde Park.

Rosen's mural is the only one in the group paid for by the Treasury Relief Artists Program, headed at the time by Olin Dows, who himself did the murals in Rhinebeck and Hyde Park. Unlike the Treasury's Section of Fine Arts, TRAP, administered the Treasury Department but which the WPA funded, required between ten to twenty-five percent of the artists it sponsored to be eligible for relief. For the Section, which funded the other murals in the group, it was either a matter of being chosen on the basis of sketches submitted, or less frequently, on winning a competition.

An artist and Harvard classmate of FDR, George Biddle, is credited with inspiring the New Deal's employment of artists, with another artist, lawyer, and Treasury Department administrator, Edward Bruce, given credit for implementing the first federal program. For this, Biddle gathered support from other Treasury officials, and from Secretary Morgenthau's wife, Elinor, as well as from Eleanor Roosevelt.[17] Elinor Morgenthau also played a significant role as the president's intermediary, bringing his wishes about the art and architecture of these Mid-Hudson Valley post offices to the attention of Edward Bruce and C. J. Peoples, Treasury's director of procurement. On one occasion, in August 1936, Elinor Morgenthau and Eleanor Roosevelt went together to visit Charles Rosen in his Woodstock studio to see his sketches for the Beacon murals. The First Lady reported on their visit in her column, "My Day," saying they "spent a delightful time in his studio. The map he is painting, which is to go the length of the lobby, is not only lovely in color, but interesting in design. The other paintings harmonize in color and give additional views which are historically interesting as well as scenically."[18]

Historical accuracy and realism were hallmarks of the murals in this distinctive cluster of New Deal post offices. In Beacon, one could stand in the lobby and readily identify local sights in the murals, such as the Beacon-Newburgh ferry (Pl. IIa). This is the same ferry that brought FDR from Beacon to Newburgh for another traditional election-eve

BOTTOM: Section of pictorial map depicting "Vassar College Library POUGHKEEP-SIE" and "Home of Franklin D. Roosevelt HYDE PARK."

BELOW: Postcard views of the Vassar College Library and home of Franklin D. Roosevelt, Hyde Park.

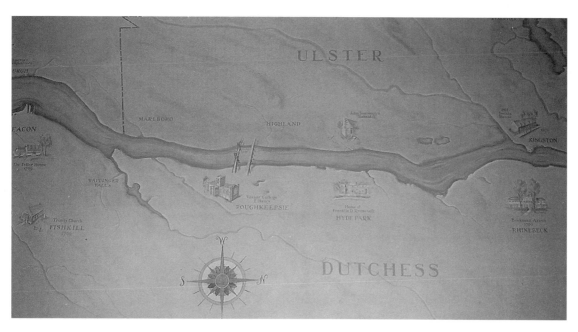

stop where he once remarked, "I feel like a bridegroom just now because when I got off the ferry someone showered me with rice."[19] But for all of the post office murals influenced by the president, it was a particular kind of realism that allowed for no negativity. There was no hint, for example, that America was in the depths of a Great Depression. There was no suggestion of social unrest in Beacon, even though the workers in the hat factory depicted in the lobby were out on strike the day that the post office opened. Many New Deal murals in post offices across America were positive in outlook, although a few were realistic in more negative terms, but not in the Mid-Hudson Valley. The message in the Beacon murals and in others in the group seems to be hope born of pride of place.

OPPOSITE

The Wappingers Falls Police Station and VIllage Hall was formerly the Wappingers Falls Post Office. It is located at 2628 South Avenue.

THE STAMP OF FDR

Wappingers Falls: Uniquely Styled

THE NEXT POST OFFICE in the chain is in Wappingers Falls, a village some ten miles north of Beacon. This small, one-story post office, whose cornerstone was laid in 1939, differs from Beacon in having a thoroughly domestic cast. The lack of a cupola, and the addition of brick chimneys, attractive pale blue shutters and a mock divided Dutch door with colonial hardware promotes this effect. Built at a cost of only $50,000, the post office uses less expensive materials in the lobby to great advantage. Wooden floors and paneled walls and window recesses, and hand hewn beams supporting the gabled ceiling all contribute to the appealing interior. Murals in the

THE STAMP OF FDR

gables at either end add an important decorative element to the high-ceilinged lobby.

The post office in Wappingers Falls is unique within the group in echoing the design of a house that still stands. The architecture refers to the Brouwer-Mesier house in a park across the way, built by Nicholas Brouwer about 1750, and added on to by the next owner, Peter Mesier, in 1777, and by others at a later date. While the reference is apparent, it is not exact. Most notably, the Mesier House is wooden and the post office is fieldstone with brick gables at each end. The post office itself has had a gabled entrance porch added in recent years.

Rudolph Stanley-Brown: Architect of Choice for FDR

Rudolph Stanley-Brown was the government architect for this building, having left private practice in Cleveland to work in the Roosevelt New Deal. It was a mutually satisfactory arrangement. Once Stanley-Brown did the post office in Rhinebeck in 1938, which pleased Roosevelt immensely, he became the choice of architect for the final three buildings in the Mid-Hudson group. This well-educated architect, who studied at Yale and Columbia and at the Ècole des Beaux-Arts in Paris, shared the president's enthusiasm for historic architecture. He was willing to pursue architectural sources and materials in Dutchess and Ulster Counties when necessary, and to follow up on every detail. It was a comfortable relationship between Stanley-Brown and FDR, encouraged from the beginning by informal Sunday night suppers at the White House, with the First Lady cooking scrambled eggs for the new group of architects and the president putting them at ease by making jokes. The setting was perhaps less intimidating to Stanley-Brown than to some of the others, since he was the grandson of another president, James A. Garfield.[20]

The All-Pervasive Role of FDR

There is no question that FDR played a decisive role in the design of the post office in Wappingers Falls. The architectural historian William Rhoads chronicles it well, beginning with Roosevelt informing Admiral Peoples, director of procurement, that the building was to be designed according to his wishes. He had already decided on the Brouwer-Mesier house as the model. Roosevelt wanted the post office to be situated in a park adjacent to Zion Episcopal Church, but the parishioners opposed the idea.

OPPOSITE

TOP: Mesier House–eighteenth century with later modifications.

BOTTOM: Wappingers Falls Post Office before the addition of porch.

FDR bowed to their wishes and settled on a corner site just south of the church and the park instead. The result is actually an attractive arrangement of buildings and parks. The post office faces onto Zion Park across South Street, while being overlooked from East Main Street by the prerevolutionary house it derives from sitting on a rise in Mesier Park. Stanley-Brown was given some license in selecting North River bluestone from a local quarry, which he had laid up in the manner of the fireplace backing of the Mesier house. Roosevelt approved the finished product. The president had intended to speak at the dedication of the post office on May 18, 1940, but Hitler's invasion of the Low Countries and France kept the president in Washington.[21]

Two Views of Wappingers Falls: Henry Billings, Muralist

A Rhinebeck artist, Henry Billings (b. 1901) painted two views of the impressive gorge and falls on Wappinger Creek, only a short downhill walk from the building, seen from the same vantage point a hundred years apart. The

OPPOSITE: Rudolph Stanley-Brown, Architect.
(Katherine Stanley-Brown Abbott)

BELOW: Preliminary sketch of Wappingers Falls Post Office on the first site chosen near Zion Episcopal Church.
(Franklin D. Roosevelt Library)

THE STAMP OF FDR

murals are entitled *First Mill on Wappinger Creek, 1780* (Pl. IIIa) and *Textile Mill in Wappingers Falls,* 1880. Billings painted the scenes directly onto chestnut panels by presidential request. Roosevelt would have preferred the first scene to be a portrayal of the Wappinger Indians around 1650, but Helen Wilkinson Reynolds persuaded him to use the 1780 scene instead. The artist signed the earlier of the two murals on the lower right, "Henry Billings 1940."

Henry Billings was an established artist of some distinction, with work in the Whitney Museum of American Art and at Rockefeller Center. He also taught at Bard College. Billings's friend Olin Dows, who included his portrait in his own post office murals in Rhinebeck, characterized Billings as "a socially conscious modern painter"[22] (Pl. IIIb). The paired murals of the same scene provide continuity of place, as well as a sense of change, as the scene moves from the eighteenth century and two men surveying the first water-powered mills on that site and a charming covered bridge to the nineteenth century, where a stone bridge has replaced the wooden one, and substantial textile mills have taken the place of the early saw mills beside the falls. The earlier scene was inspired by notes in the diary of the Marquis de Chastellux, shown standing in conversation with Peter Mesier, whose house the post office architecture alludes to. The French general officer en route from

THE STAMP OF FDR

Newburgh to Saratoga in December 1780 wrote that he stopped some moments at the Fall of Wapping "to take in, under different points of view, the charming landscape which that stream forms as much by its cascade, which is rushing and picturesque, as by the groups of trees and of rocks, which united with the saw mills and other mills made a picture most pleasing and agreeable."[23]

President Roosevelt held a news conference from his car at the site of the new Wappingers Falls post office on 18 November 1939, asking the reporters: "Are you ready to do some architectural reporting today?"[24] He began by pointing out that this post office differs from some others in that the end gables are brick, justifying this by saying it was one of the standard ways to build an old house. The president devoted a good deal of the news conference to explaining what the decoration inside was going to be like, and providing some historical background. He started with the mention of Wappinger Creek close by, the main center of the Wappinger tribe of Indians, from whom the creek took its name. The first picture will show how the falls looked when the Marquis de Chastellux came through to join Rochambeau's army on the way to the siege of Yorktown. He then proceeded to fill in more Revolutionary War history. The second picture will be the same scene, from the same spot, taken from an old painting about 1850, "when this was a very big and very important manufacturing center, literally, with cotton mills and the water power all harnessed." A reporter commented: "The town does not look any too prosperous," to which FDR replied: "It is a lot better than it used to be ten years or twenty years ago."

The murals as rendered are, in effect, idyllic scenes. The only figures in the first picture are Peter Mesier and the Marquis de Chastellux talking quietly beside the gorge. No one connected with the mills is rendered in either scene. In the second picture, small images of a jauntily-dressed fisherman in a boater hat at the far left and a similarly-dressed man seated on a ledge at the right, peacefully observing youthful swimmers down below, constitute the only human activity. Despite being an artist concerned with social realism, Henry Billings has given no hint of a mill town that does not look too prosperous. Only scenes from the past, and not the present, have been depicted. However, as William Rhoads has observed, the historic renditions of harnessed water-power put to industrial uses are meant to be seen as forerunners of the impressive water-power projects of the Roosevelt New Deal. Public works such as the completion of Boulder Dam during Roosevelt's administration were as important to this president as his more local interests in Dutchess County.[25]

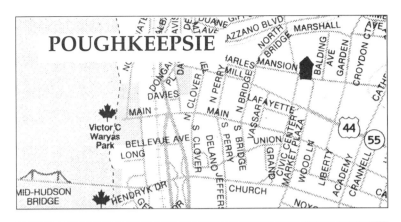

Poughkeepsie Post Office located at 55 Mansion Street.

Cast bronze bell in Poughkeepsie cupola with inscription chosen by FDR

THE STAMP OF FDR

Poughkeepsie: Premier Post Office in the Mid-Hudson Valley

BY ANY MEASURE, Poughkeepsie is the group's premier post office (Pl. IV). The building, completed in 1938, cost far more than any of the others: $300,000 plus $110,000 to secure the site, with extra fees for a landscaping consultant from New York. Roosevelt himself ordered a cast bronze bell for the copper-domed cupola, at a cost of $4,569.[26] The lobby murals executed by three separate artists totaled more than $13,000–over four times the normal one percent of the total expense reserved for interior decoration. The result was an outstanding architectural and artistic achievement that has stood well the test of time.

Roosevelt actually had even more ambitious architectural plans than the handsome post office building. He thought ahead to the creation of a civic plaza. In his dedication speech in 1938, FDR referred to a deceased Poughkeepsie realtor, James E. Sague, who had effected an extension of Market Street and who dreamed of a beautiful building commanding the head of the street with a vista extending over many blocks. The post office fulfilled Sague's dream. Roosevelt recommended the site for a second civic building, the Poughkeepsie Newspaper Building, at right angles to the post office, erected in 1941. He encouraged the owner, Merritt C. Speidel, in his penchant for colonial design, and because of FDR, the walls were of stone locally acquired.[27] A grateful Speidel presented the president with a large architectural rendering of the Poughkeepsie "News Cathedral," so-called, with an inscription applauding his vision in the planning of the Poughkeepsie post office as the first structure in a civic group. At a 1941 press conference, Roosevelt called for a new city hall on the opposite corner from the Newspaper

NEWS CATHEDRAL POUGHKEEPSIE NEWSPAPERS

This Rendering Was Made Especially For Our Good Neighbor And Friend The First Citizen Of Dutchess County

HYDE PARK   FRANKLIN D. ROOSEVELT   NEW YORK

Presented By His Friend MERRITT C. SPEIDEL *In Grateful Acknowledgement Of His Many Helpful And Constructive Suggestions For The Design And Materials Used In This Building For His Deep Interest In Preserving For Posterity The Traditional Architecture Of The Hudson Valley And In Recognition Of His Vision In The Planning Of* THE UNITED STATES POST OFFICE *In Poughkeepsie New York As The First Structure Of This Civic Group Sept. 1941.*

ABOVE: Rendering of Pough-keepsie "News Cathedral" commissioned by Merritt C. Speidel especially for Franklin D. Roosevelt.

(Franklin D. Roosevelt Library)

OPPOSITE

LEFT: Bronze tablet at entrance to Poughkeepsie Post Office.

RIGHT: Bronze sconce with eagle on Poughkeepsie facade.

BELOW: Blueprint of sconce displayed in the lobby.

Building to complete the plaza. It went without saying that the city hall should be fieldstone, like the post office and the Newspaper Building. A third matching building to complete the president's plan never materialized.[28]

It is no wonder that Poughkeepsie received special favor. It was not only the county seat of Roosevelt's beloved Dutchess County, full of history which he himself knew well, but it was also the seat of the Dutchess County Democratic Party. Roosevelt's political career officially began in Poughkeepsie when he was endorsed as the party's candidate for State Senator at the county convention there on October 6, 1910. It began unofficially in Poughkeepsie two months before when, as he tells it, he ran into a group of friends in front of the courthouse who took him to a policeman's picnic where he made his first speech. FDR perceived that chance encounter in Pough-keepsie and its consequences as a watershed event. Twenty-three years later, in August 1933, he reported on the event that changed his life to an audience in Poughkeepsie at Vassar College.[29]

Eric Kebbon, Architect

The architect for the Poughkeepsie post office, Eric Kebbon, brought a good deal of experience to the task. After gradu-

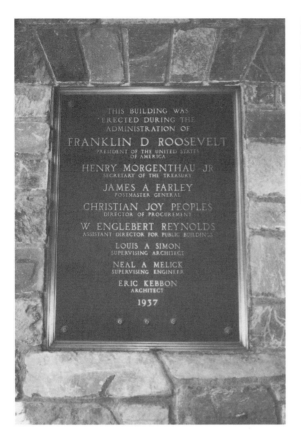

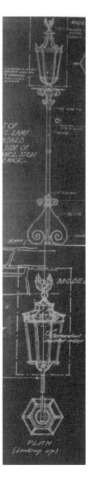

ating from the Massachusetts Institute of Technology in 1912 and studying abroad, he returned to his alma mater as resident architect. Kebbon worked in New York City as an associate of Welles Bosworth, where he was in charge of plans for the American Telephone and Telegraph Building. He was in private practice from 1921 to 1938, meanwhile joining the temporary staff of the Office of the Supervising Architect designing post offices. In 1938, he was appointed to the Board of Education of the City of New York, designing over one hundred schools for the city before he left that post in 1951. Unfortunately, Kebbon's stellar architectural background was not well suited for the demands of FDR. His work was too sophisticated for simple vernacular Dutch Colonial architecture. He wanted to use fine quarried bluestone, when the president wanted native stone collected from fields around Poughkeepsie. The president asked to see a sample layup of the stone walls, which he firmly rejected, sending Kebbon to look at the walls of the James Roosevelt Memorial Library in Hyde Park. (See page 6.) FDR argued against Kebbon's formal touches, such as keystones in the arched openings and horizontal belt courses to clarify the divisions between stories. FDR evidently approved of some of Kebbon's elegant touches, such as outdoor wall sconces and standing lamps embossed with bronze eagles flanking the recessed entryway. But his work never quite won the heart of the president from Dutchess County, who had his own architectural vision.

Layers of Meaning for FDR in the Design of the Post Office

FDR made it clear that he wanted the Poughkeepsie post office to be based on a Dutchess County courthouse built in 1809, a building that once stood only two blocks away from the proposed post office. He commissioned his fellow historian in Poughkeepsie Helen Wilkinson Reynolds to find an old photograph of the courthouse to guide the architect. The principal correspondence between the two buildings derives from long, two-story elevations with comparable arched openings, and cupolas with octagonal domes. One notable difference is that the walls of the early building appear to be smooth surfaces and may even have been stuccoed, according to Miss Reynolds. What is missing is the salient feature of fieldstone.

The Dutchess County Courthouse of 1809 had great significance to FDR as being a replacement for one on the same site where a convention of New York delegates met to ratify the Federal Constitution in 1788. He believed it possible that some walls of the 1780s courthouse may have been incorporated into the courthouse of 1809. Roosevelt

Prototype for the Poughkeepsie Post Office: Dutchess County Court House ca. 1809
(Dutchess County Historical Society)

THE STAMP OF FDR

spoke of the importance of the momentous convention when he dedicated the Poughkeepsie post office and laid the cornerstone on October 13, 1937. He told of a terrific struggle between the Clintonians and the Hamiltonians as to whether New York State should ratify the Constitution without a Bill of Rights. A Dutchess County delegate named Melancthon Smith proposed a compromise: that New York ratify the Constitution in full faith that a Bill of Rights would be forthcoming. As the former governor of New York, the president might well have taken extra pride in what happened in Poughkeepsie in 1788, when Poughkeepsie was the capital of New York State.

FDR noted at the dedication that his great-great-grandfather had been a member of that convention, but admittedly as a member of the Hamiltonian faction that "said that it (a Bill of Rights) did not make much difference."[30] A large mural in the upper lobby of the post office records the presence of FDR's ancestor Isaac Roosevelt in the courthouse scene at the moment of compromise when Governor Clinton and Alexander Hamilton shake hands. Isaac Roosevelt is readily recognizable from his portrait by Gilbert Stuart furnished as a model by the president (Pl.Va). The portrait took pride of place over the mantel in the drawing room of the Roosevelt family home in Hyde Park (Pl. Vb). Roosevelt clearly shared his family's pride in

President Roosevelt lays the cornerstone for the Poughkeepsie Post Office, October 13, 1937.

(Franklin D. Roosevelt Library)

Poughkeepsie: Premier Post Office in the Mid-Hudson Valley

their eighteenth-century ancestor who helped establish the federal government.

Franklin Roosevelt was under attack for New Deal measures said to be in violation of the Constitution. Rhoads makes the astute suggestion that the mural celebrating New York's ratification of the Constitution, with Isaac Roosevelt prominently involved, is intended to give prima facie evidence that FDR strongly supports the U.S. Constitution.[31] Indeed, support of the Constitution is almost in his blood. FDR would, however, be on the side of the Antifederalists in seeing the importance of a Bill of Rights with its guarantees of personal freedom. Freedom was a byword for this president ever since his first Inaugural Address. The inscription he devised for the bronze bell in the post office cupola reads: "Ring the Perpetuation of American Freedom." The architectural allusions to the former Courthouse in Poughkeepsie, the courthouse scene in the lobby, and the bell in the tower with its cast bronze inscription combine to make a calculated statement for FDR.

An Opulent Example of Classic Modernism

The monumental Poughkeepsie post office is in some respects like a Beacon post office blown large. It has the same federal cast on the outside, heightened by an eagle emblazoned on a classical white pediment outlined with dentils; but in this case the eagle clutches bound fasces in its talons, a symbol of the Republic borrowed from Rome. The expansive, two-story lobby in Poughkeepsie displays a

Poughkeepsie lobby faced with marble and polished bronze, looking east towards Charles Rosen's "View of the City of Poughkeepsie c.1939."

THE STAMP OF FDR

plethora of variegated green and white marble reminiscent of the smaller post office down the river (Pl. VI). In Poughkeepsie, even side tables in the lobby are made of this luxurious material. The first floor and the wraparound mezzanine are indicated separately by marble columns changing from Doric to Ionic on the upper level. Burnished bronze is used extensively to create a similarly opulent effect, including decorative fluted panels and a large coffered door to the office of the postmaster. At the same time, a modern note is struck by hanging satellite light fixtures and geometric grilles and railings on the balcony and the stairs that lead up to it. The open public interior is a pleasing example of classic modernism—a popular choice for federal buildings in America in the 1930s and 1940s.

The Mystery of the Tunnel

The sizeable post office in Poughkeepsie did more than house the Postal Service. The original tenants of the building included the Department of Agriculture, the Civil Service, the F.B.I., the Navy, the Army, and the Marine Corps. Tenants of this type may have been the reason for an unusual feature of the building—a tunnel in the basement leading to the National Armory a block away.

The post office did not open until December 1938, when war in Europe was clearly on the horizon. The need to protect the president of the United States in case of emergency might well have helped to determine a monumental stone edifice housing all of the Armed Forces and the F.B.I., with an underground tunnel to an armory with ready access to the Hudson River where warships could dock. A "one-passenger elevator," according to the inventory, in the work area away from the public going down to where the tunnel begins is also suggestive. Given Roosevelt's awareness of the possibility of war, and his status as commander in chief, the tunnel as a security measure seems like a reasonable explanation.

Murals by
Gerald Foster, Georgina Klitgaard, and
Charles Rosen—A History of Poughkeepsie
from Beginning to End

Five large murals in the two-story lobby executed by three individual artists chronicle the history of Poughkeepsie from beginning to end. In his speech at the post office ded-

ication, the secretary of the Treasury Henry Morgenthau Jr. noted that President Roosevelt had personally selected the subjects of the murals. Westfield, New Jersey, artist Gerald Foster painted the first three canvasses on the walls of the second floor gallery, signing each one in the lower right hand corner: "Gerald Foster 1938." A Princeton graduate who had studied at the Art Students League and in Paris and in Rome, Foster was known as an ardent student of the Revolutionary War period. He had already done a historic mural for the Section in Freehold, New Jersey, in 1935-1936.[32] Foster seems to have been selected for Poughkeepsie without a formal competition. FDR might have been favorably disposed towards this artist because he was a painter of boats. In any event, Gerald Foster received $8,000 for the three Poughkeepsie murals, the highest fee paid to an artist in the public buildings program.

THE STAMP OF FDR

"Poughkeepsie circa 1692"

Gerald Foster, "Poughkeepsie
c. 1692"

The series begins on the east wall with a scene showing a meeting of Dutchmen and Wappinger Indians in 1692 in the woods by a stream and a waterfall at a place that gave Poughkeepsie its name. The Indian name for Poughkeepsie, Apokeepsing, translates as "reed covered lodge by the little watering place," something indicated in the scene. Roosevelt was generally pleased with Foster's sketch for the mural, but he returned it with a note stating two objections. Horses would not have been present in the scene at this early date, and some of the trees were too thin for a primordial forest; they looked like second growth. Foster fattened the trees and removed the animals forthwith.

Roosevelt's attention to the mural and the depth of his knowledge greatly impressed Edward Bruce, chief of the

Section of Fine Arts. In January 1940, Bruce wrote to General Edwin M. Watson at the White House asking if the president would let him come over with a photographer from *Life* magazine to take a picture of the president going over Henry Billings's designs for Wappingers Falls to illustrate the great interest the president takes in the decorations of federal buildings. He also wrote: "I am keen to quote the famous note of the President that in 1640 there were no horses or second growth timber at the mouth of the Apokeepsing Creek." As Bruce said, "It is a grand story."[33]

"Hamlet of Poughkeepsie c. 1750"

THE SECOND MURAL in chronological sequence appears on the opposite west wall (Pl. VI). "Hamlet of Poughkeepsie c. 1750" is a simplified scene made up of three buildings of significance at the time: the Reformed Dutch Church, a farmhouse/tavern, and a new fieldstone courthouse, the second to occupy the site since Poughkeepsie was made county seat in 1714. Also depicted are some typical inhabitants on foot and on horseback, and travelers in a stagecoach making a stop along the King's Highway. The choice of fieldstone buildings exclusively, with nothing of wood to be seen, lends architectural support to the implicit idea that the new fieldstone post office of 1937 maintains continuity with the past without interruption.

THE STAMP OF FDR

Bells are another unifying link between past and present. The church bell in the mural rang to announce the arrival of mail brought at uncertain times by sloop, rider, or stage, the means chosen for the wall painting. The bell also tolled to notify residents of important events, as was the case during the Ratification Convention of 1788. The bell in the cupola of this post office building was a meaningful link with what went on in the eighteenth century in Poughkeepsie. The bell intended to "ring the perpetuation of American freedom" continues to toll for certain significant events, as it did for the bicentennial celebration of the adoption of the Constitution in 1988.

"July 26, 1788, New York State Ratifies the United States Constitution in the Dutchess County Court House in Poughkeepsie"

The Ratification scene occupies the long north wall facing the entrance to the building. But unlike the murals at either end, this one is hard to see from the lobby downstairs. The best view of all three is from the balcony which can be reached by one of two marble and bronze staircases beside the two glass-enclosed vestibules at the entrance. The murals are not well placed for viewing, in that the balconies are too shallow to allow one to step back for an overall look.

Gerald Foster, "July 26, 1788 New York State Ratifies the United States Constitution in the Dutchess County Court House in Poughkeepsie."
(Franklin D. Roosevelt Library)

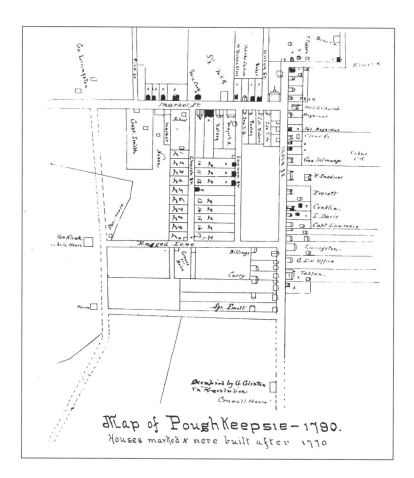

"Map of Poughkeepsie—1780."
(Adriance Memorial Library, reproduced in Foster's Ratification mural)

The courthouse room where the scene is set reflects the preferences of the president and his associate Helen Wilkinson Reynolds–a simple interior furnished with authentically correct Dutchess County furniture and benches of the period, with the only wall decoration a map of Poughkeepsie dated 1780. The framed map by the window manages to evoke associations with a Dutch interior and an American colonial interior simultaneously. The artist aimed for authenticity in his figural depictions as well. Besides Isaac Roosevelt, Foster painted likenesses of Melancton Smith, George Clinton, Alexander Hamilton, John Jay, and Robert R. Livingston. For the rest, he had to improvise. He used his assistant John Poehler, for Richard Morris, seated at the far right. In turn, Poehler painted Foster's face on Cornelius Schoonmaker, the only participant facing away from the momentous handshake taking place at the center.[34]

John Poehler decided to add a mouse looking out from a hole in the baseboard directly beneath the extended handshake. Foster reported that it was just a gag which "we figured would delight any school children touring the post office."[35] The amusing addition has delighted children of all ages ever since. The mouse and mousehole also

THE STAMP OF FDR

reveal the hand of an expert designer. The crux of the picture, the critical handshake, is emphasized by taking place across an empty space in front of a plain background. The little dark mousehole standing out in the lighter baseboard adds to the emphatic arrangement by being part of a vertical axis moving up from the end of a sharply-pointed step to the hole to the fall of Governor Clinton's ruffled cuff overhead.

Paired scenes of Poughkeepsie at opposite ends of the lower lobby measure almost seventeen feet across, covering the entire width of the wall between marble pilasters. Painted by Georgina Klitgaard and Charles Rosen in 1940, who won out over eighteen artists in a competition open to all American artists who were residents of or attached to Dutchess or Ulster Counties, they depict the same view of Poughkeepsie from across the Hudson River in 1839 and 1939 respectively. Both artists signed their canvases at the lower right, but only Rosen added a date. Seafoam green is the predominant color in each mural, conferring another dimension of unity to the paired river views of the city. The pale green hue also serves to integrate the wall paintings with the pale green marble interior.

Gerald Foster, detail of the critical handshake above a mouse hole in the baseboard.

"View of the Village of Poughkeepsie in 1839"

Georgina Klitgaard (1893-1976) who painted the mural on the west wall, was born in Spuyten Duyvil, New York, and studied at Barnard College and the National Academy of Design. Klitgaard lived near Woodstock for a number of years and was considered one of America's leading landscape artists. She won prizes from the Pennsylvania Academy and the Chicago Art Institute, and her works are in the Whitney Museum of American Art and the Metropolitan Museum of Art, among others. Klitgaard had already done a smaller mural for the post office in Goshen, New York, in 1937, but not without a certain amount of controversy. After visiting Goshen and talking with the people there, she concluded that "The Running of the Hambletonian Stake," the famous trotting race in Goshen, would be an appropriate subject, but Section officials did not. Klitgaard finally had her way.[36]

President Roosevelt himself furnished a mid-nineteenth century print for the artist to follow, asking that Poughkeepsie's highest point, College Hill, be added to the scene, atop which sat Poughkeepsie Collegiate School, a boys' school Roosevelt's father had attended. He was generally accepting of Klitgaard's rendition of Poughkeepsie in 1839 with its busy waterfront lined with warehouses and businesses, such as the Vassar Brewery, and streets leading up the hill past commercial and residential areas to the Dutch Reformed and Episcopal Churches, and the all-important 1809 courthouse, referred to architecturally. What did not please the president was the artist's rendition of some of the boats carrying cargo and passengers on the river. FDR objected to Edward Bruce that the whaling ship on the left was "pretty terrible," the two steamboats were too long because of an error in perspective, and "the wind in the sails of the four sail boats is coming from four different points of the compass."[37] Thus speaks the voice of a man whose extensive knowledge and lifelong love of boats was a defining characteristic.

Klitgaard worked under the tutelage of Roosevelt's consultant, Helen Wilkinson Reynolds, who, according to the artist in a newspaper interview some years later, "became my personal friend during that project." Miss Reynolds "knew old Poughkeepsie," and taught Klitgaard to know Poughkeepsie better. "She wanted more of her beloved Poughkeepsie in the mural. So I put more of it in, even the little garden her family had down by the river."[38]

Klitgaard added something of her own to the waterfront scene that made a real contribution to the painting. As

Karal Ann Marling observed, she used idioms of American art in the nineteenth century to make direct reference to the historical period. "The crisp neoprimitive renderings of the boats, the luminous absence of atmospheric perspective, and the blasted Hudson River School tree branch are stylistic quotations from the epoch pictured. Such nuances help to emphasize the remoteness of the historical past." Beyond this, "The primal clarity and innocence with which reality is perceived make a familiar place suddenly unfamiliar enough to warrant renewed interest"[39] (Pl. VII).

"View of the City of Poughkeepsie circa 1939"

Time moves forward a hundred years in Charles Rosen's mural on the opposite wall, bringing the sight of the city of Poughkeepsie into what was then the present (Pl. VIII). His was a particularly accomplished mural with its multiple perspectives. The painting calls to mind some cubist landscapes of Paul Cezanne. The city on the hill is now bustling with commerce and industry. High rise buildings are beginning to appear in the center, near the successor to the eighteenth-century courthouse erected in 1904 and the New Deal post office at center left. Different types of boats

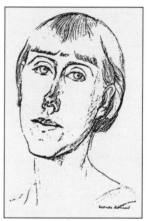

ABOVE: Georgina Klitgaard, self-portrait, pencil on paper, 1940.
(Woodstock Artists Association Archives)

TOP: Post Office lobby looking west towards Klitgaard's "View of the Village of Poughkeepsie in 1839."

now populate the river, among them a small pleasure craft and a dayliner for passenger excursions. Long sculls across the wide horizontal expanse are participating in the famous Poughkeepsie Regatta, a race that for generations drew the top oarsmen from large eastern colleges. Two bridges now span the Hudson River: the Poughkeepsie Railroad Bridge (1889) and the Mid-Hudson Bridge (1930). Again, as in Beacon and Wappingers Falls, there is no inkling of economic hardship in this city in 1939.

Franklin Roosevelt believed in government-sponsored public works, for the service they provided and for what they did for the nation's economy. The little image of the new post office included in the scene testifies to his beliefs and to his political patronage. Roosevelt was especially proud of major public works like the Mid-Hudson Bridge, begun by Al Smith but completed when Roosevelt was governor of New York. Eleanor Roosevelt cut the ribbon for the opening. The beautifully constructed bridge looming out from the right in an encompassing arc that takes up a third of the canvas becomes a metaphor for the protective arm of the Roosevelt New Deal and a symbol of hope for the future.

The whole cycle of murals going back to Poughkeepsie's beginnings in 1692 and moving up through history to the immediate present, as witnessed by an image of a brand new post office, offers a sense of security for those living through a Great Depression. Unbroken continuity

OPPOSITE: Trowel President Roosevelt used to lay the cornerstone on display in the Poughkeepsie Post Office.

BELOW: Matted Photo, "View of the City of Poughkeepsie c. 1939," signed "Charles Rosen-'40."

(Franklin D. Roosevelt Library)

THE STAMP OF FDR

with the past, and a past of significant accomplishments, acts as a guarantee for a brighter future. Poughkeepsie more than most exemplifies what Marling calls "the futurological orientation" of New Deal history painting.[40] The person most responsible for the whole conception of the Poughkeepsie post office, Franklin D. Roosevelt, would have known he was leaving a legacy of hope there for future generations.

The Gift of the Trowel

FDR made the legacy he left in Poughkeepsie quite explicit. The Poughkeepsie postmaster Charles I. Lavery received a letter from the acting director of the Franklin D. Roosevelt Library in Hyde Park, Edgar B. Nixon, written on January 1, 1944, stating that the president wished to give the trowel he used at the laying of the cornerstone on October 13, 1937, to the Poughkeepsie post office.[41] This tangible evidence of a new post office in Poughkeepsie and the president's role in bringing it about is still on display over fifty years later in a glass case on the lobby wall, bearing the explanatory engraving: "This trowel was presented to Franklin D Roosevelt, President of the United States October 13, 1937 for the purpose of setting the cornerstone of the post office building. Poughkeepsie, NY by William J. Moore, Construction Eng."

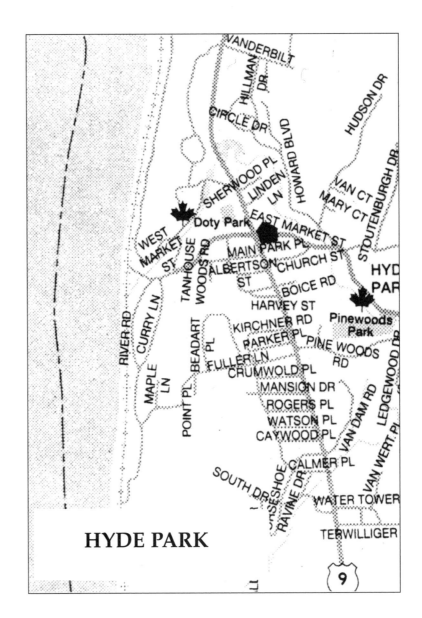

Hyde Park Post Office located at 1 East Market Street.

THE STAMP OF FDR

Hyde Park:
Post Office and
Agricultural Building

Franklin D. Roosevelt

THE HYDE PARK POST OFFICE is only five miles up the Hudson from Poughkeepsie on the Albany Post Road (Route 9). The post office and what was originally an agricultural building took as its model the home of an illustrious citizen of Hyde Park, Dr. John Bard. (Pl. IX) The president's Poughkeepsie lawyer Henry Hackett and his friend and fellow historian Helen Wilkinson Reynolds suggested the Bard house.[42] The wooden house built about 1772 was an appropriate choice for several reasons. As President Roosevelt explained in his speech at the post office dedication on November 6, 1940, John Bard's grandfather was the original patentee of Hyde Park. Bard's estate, which Roosevelt described as "probably the oldest estate in the North that has been kept up as an estate for nearly 200 years," was named Hyde Park "in honor of the Hyde family—Lord Clarendon in England at that time." In turn, Bard's Hyde Park estate gave its name to the village.

Olin Dows, mural, Drs. John and Samuel Bard examine the results of an agricultural experiment in the late 1780s.
(Franklin D. Roosevelt Library)

45

Roosevelt described Bard himself as "a very great naturalist."[43] As illustration, a scene in the post office murals shows Dr. Bard and his son, Dr. Samuel Bard, examining one of their experiments: imported Italian melons fertilized with gypsum. The label beneath the scene goes on to say: "These two men were New York's most distinguished physicians." Dr. John Bard was the first president of the New York Medical Society. He performed the first dissection for instruction, and the first diagnosis and successful operation for extra uterine pregnancy recorded in the colonies. He also fought the public health menace, yellow fever, recommending Bedloe's Island as a quarantine station. Dr. Samuel Bard's medical credentials, according to the label, include study in Edinburgh before founding the Medical School of Kings College, later the College of Physicians and Surgeons, where he was the first professor of medicine and president. He also was the first to agitate for a hospital. As a naturalist, Samuel Bard encouraged local horticultural improvements, such as the use of clover as a crop. In 1806, he became the first president of the Society of Dutchess County for the Promotion of Agriculture. It seems eminently appropriate that a building that housed an agricultural station as well as a post office was based on the home of Dr. John Bard.

Bard's house was destroyed in 1875. Roosevelt asked his mother to locate a picture of the house at the James Roosevelt Library, but she could not. Instead, she came up with a pen and ink sketch by a local antiquarian Edward Braman to serve as a model. Architect Rudolph Stanley-Brown followed Braman's sketch quite closely, producing an attractive two-story building with hipped roof underlined by a dentilated cornice and one-story wings at either side. The only obvious change was to move the entrance over from right to left. A white pedimented porch shelters the entrance, with a paneled door inset with glass and a geometrically-sectioned transom. Stanley-Brown's Hyde Park post office, like his earlier building in Wappingers Falls, has gabled ends with clapboard siding and twelve-over-twelve sash windows with pale blue shutters. Hand-blown window panes add an authentic touch to the structure. The main fabric of the building, fieldstone, came from walls running through a farm owned by Maud Stoutenburgh Eliot on property once owned by Dr. Samuel Bard. Her ancestor, Jacobus Stoutenburgh, built the first stone house in the village in 1745. Before construction began, a sample stone wall twelve feet long and five feet high was erected on the site for the president's inspection.[44] On the lawn to the left of the entrance is a white, latticed well head requested by Roosevelt who believed the original Bard

THE STAMP OF FDR

"The Red House". Built 1772 - by Dr. John Bard.

house had had this type of "old oaken bucket well."[45] As a result, the whole post office complex on the corner lot presents a domestic colonial scene full of vintage charm.

Olin Dows—Artist for the Occasion

Olin Dows (1904-1981) painted a continuous frieze on the upper walls of the post office lobby detailing three hundred years of Hyde Park history in 1941. Dows was uniquely qualified to do so. He was qualified as an artist, as a lifelong resident of nearby Rhinebeck, where he had executed a similar mural in the post office lobby the year before, and as someone who rivaled the president in his knowledge of and love for the Hudson River landscape and local history. His grandfather, along with FDR, had been a founding member of the Dutchess County Historical Society. He was part of a neighboring River family, with the same pride in his ancestors, some of whom, like the Beekmans in Rhinebeck, he shared with the president. His obituary described him as a very distant cousin of FDR.

Olin Dows knew that he wanted to be an artist when he was a boy. His family engaged C. K. Chatterton of Vassar College to tutor him in drawing. He attended Harvard College for two years before leaving to attend the Yale Art School. He then spent time at the Arts Students League in New York and a memorable summer in Mexico where he met the great muralist Diego Rivera. That encounter and a trip to Egypt in 1939 to visit his sister seemed to have an impact on his murals.

Dows wanted very much to paint the murals in Hyde

TOP: Hyde Park Post Office
lobby ca.1941
(Franklin D. Roosevelt Library)

ABOVE: Olin Dows ca.1937
(The Museum of Rhinebeck History)

Park, as he had in Rhinebeck. He had offered to paint the Rhinebeck murals without payment, if necessary.[46] Instead he was paid $1,000 for Rhinebeck and for Hyde Park, but his expenses totaled approximately $950 each time. That Dows would have done the murals without recompense is a measure of his beliefs. He believed in Franklin Roosevelt and the programs Roosevelt was undertaking to bring the nation back to health. As a former arts administrator, Dows was especially committed to government programs which this president was the first to initiate. In a paper he read to the Dutchess County Historical Society in 1942 that dealt with the Rhinebeck and Hyde Park murals, Dows said "the fact that we can see pictures on our walls showing our community's past and present life, adds to our sense of history. . . . Great art is a living record. . . . Most important it helps form and shape our beliefs."[47] The artist and the president saw the murals in the post offices from much the same perspective.

This artist was unusually willing to take suggestions in designing this rather complex program of interrelated panels, and to give credit where it belonged. He submitted a draft of possible subjects for the mural to FDR, who put checks or crosses in the margin beside each one.[48] It is interesting to note that Roosevelt did not want the first Birthday Ball held eleven years earlier by the local Home Club that grew into a nationwide benefit for the Infantile Paralysis

THE STAMP OF FDR

Foundation to be depicted. This reflects the same wish for privacy about his condition that FDR had always shown.

Towards the end of the project, Dows wrote a memo saying, "I am deeply indebted to President Roosevelt who from his extraordinary knowledge of local history has not only suggested a number of subjects, but has taken time to recommend improvements in both the inch scale model and the almost completed panels." Dows's memo went on to give Miss Helen Reynolds "particular thanks for very extensive help which she has generously given me from her understanding and entertaining fund of local history." He ended by thanking several artists who offered very useful criticisms, including Leon Hoosepian, who also ably transferred the cartoons to canvas. He was especially grateful to Henry Billings, who has followed the development of the murals and given him invaluable suggestions.[49] (See Pl. IIIb.)

There is, however, one recorded occasion when Dows refused a suggestion gently proffered by Rudolph Stanley-Brown. The architect wrote to the artist after seeing his model of the murals to say that he thought he had discovered an anachronism—architectural blue prints in the 1846 scene of men going over plans for a new St. James Church. Although blue printing was discovered by Hershel in 1840, as Stanley-Brown pointed out, architects still employed men to trace drawings in order to have more than one copy

TOP: Emil Tschudin & Sons, mahogany, Model of Hyde Park Post Office lobby, with Olin Dows's watercolors on paper, 1940.

(Franklin D. Roosevelt Library)

ABOVE: Olin Dows, mural, 1846—The Reverend Reuben Sherwood and Vestrymen discuss plans for a new St. James church.

as late as the close of the nineteenth century. He then explained exactly how this was done. The letter shows Stanley-Brown's careful attention to detail and his concern for historical accuracy. He added, however, that "it is not terribly important and if you want a spot of blue in that particular place I would forget all this."[50] Dows wrote back that he suspected a blueprint was an anachronism, but he put it in to keep the sky down. He planned to keep it there and make a note on the subject matter that it is incorrect. "I call that painters' license, don't you?"[51]

Eleanor Roosevelt wrote about seeing the finished murals in Mrs. Tracy Dows's living room in her syndicated column, "My Day." Olin Dows had brought them to his mother's house for their inspection. "He has certainly done a wonderful piece of historical research and they are delightful murals. I hope that a great many people will stop to see them and enjoy them, as they motor on the Albany Post road. They tell us that a good many people stop in the Rhinebeck, N.Y. post office to see the murals which Mr. Dows did there. Every time I hear that people really get pleasure out of these paintings, which have an historical interest as well as an artistic one, I rejoice, for I feel that we are adding permanently to the cultural heritage of our country."[52] The First Lady seemed to share her husband's understanding of the value of the post office murals.

The Story of Hyde Park

The story of Hyde Park unfolds on the post office walls high above the paneled dado. The story begins at the left of the entrance with a narrow panel filled with a standing Indian looking out at Henry Hudson's ship, the *Half Moon*, at anchor off Crum Elbow Point on 28 September 1609 (Pl. Xa). The erect Native American with his back to the viewer invites today's spectators to join in surveying the scene. For Roosevelt, the first panel represents the coming of the white man, the Dutch, to Hyde Park, in a manner comparable to the scene in the woods in Poughkeepsie. The Rhinebeck frieze also begins with an Indian man peering out at the Half Moon, with the same momentous implications (Pl. Xb). Clearly, the Wappinger Indians in the area meant something to FDR. Besides appearing in murals in three of the post offices, Roosevelt originally wanted them to be in Billings's mural in Wappingers Falls as well. But the coming of the Dutch to the Mid-Hudson Valley is an event without parallel to a president whose personal identity lay in his Dutch ancestry.

There are nineteen panels of varying sizes in the post

office frieze, full of identifiable people and activities in Hyde Park in previous centuries, as well as ones just recently past. Some of the scenes are a beehive of joyful activity reminiscent of a Currier and Ives. The murals unite around certain themes, such as the landscape, which changes as time passes from primeval woods to land under cultivation. Roosevelt told Olin Dows to look at the woods below his house, as they would suggest a background for the early panels.[53] To help the viewer with this wealth of subject matter, Dows wrote descriptive labels for each scene. Dows repeated the text in a packet of postcard views he created. The Hyde Park Historical Association has made available a reprint of the text in leaflet form.

Life on the River

One unmistakable theme is life on the river, beginning with the *Half Moon* at anchor in the Hudson in 1609. Fishing was clearly an important industry in the early years. A charming scene circa 1795 has a man and a woman quietly mending shad nets in the foreground, while others are engaged in loading and unloading boats of various sorts in the background (Pl. XI). In 1870, a more vigorous action takes center stage, whereby the head of Hyde Park's caviar industry, William Meier, pulls up an oversized sturgeon with some assistance. A 1878 woodcut in *Frank Leslie's Illustrated Newspaper* was obviously the basis for Dows's rendition. These shad and sturgeon fishermen tell of something unusual about the Hudson River at this point. Offshore at Hyde Park the river is up to one hundred feet deep. The Poughkeepsie Deepwater, so-called, runs for fourteen miles down river. Salt water flows under the fresh water

ABOVE: Olin Dows, mural, 1870. William Meier, head of the Hyde Park caviar industry, lands an oversized sturgeon with the assistance of Abe Atkins.

(Franklin D. Roosevelt Library)

TOP: Scene in *Frank Leslie's Illustrated Newspaper, 1878*, provides the basis for the sturgeon scene in Hyde Park.

surface in the deep trough, so that marine fish live in this unique environment, allowing for a prosperous fishing industry suggested in the river scenes.

Another river view is a conflation of time periods when racing iceboats was a popular pastime. John Roosevelt's iceboat, the *Icicle*, is under discussion in the foreground in 1886. In the middle ground, the lateen-rigged *Hawk* built for a young Franklin D. Roosevelt is just starting out. Finally, modern iceboats appear in the background. It is no surprise that the president found fault with the rigging and other details of the iceboats. Dows invited him to dinner to show him the full-size cartoons with the errors corrected.[54]

Slavery in Hyde Park

In writing about early Hyde Park in 1939, Henry Hackett noted that the Bards, Hosacks, McVickars, and Pendletons owned slaves. "The negroes cleared the land, dug the ditches, built the stone walls and did most of the hard work."[55] The murals testify to Hackett's observations. In a scene set before 1741, Dows's label states: "Jacobus Stoutenburgh, his sons and slaves clear the land." In the late 1780s panel, where Drs. John and Samuel Bard examine their new melons, slaves are up on ladders picking fruit, but without mention in the text. More interesting is the fact that slaves built stone walls in Hyde Park in the colonial period and might well have built the walls on Bard's property that were reused for the New Deal post office. Schooling for slave children was evidently provided in 1789, although segregated, as a black school and a white school are rendered in the background of the sturgeon fishing scene.[56]

Olin Dows, mural—Before 1741. Jacobus Stoutenburgh, his sons and slaves clear the land.

(Franklin D. Roosevelt Library)

THE STAMP OF FDR

Hackett comments that at one time, there were over sixty black families living in and about Hyde Park. His count may extend beyond 1827, when slavery was legally outlawed in New York State. In the scene where the minister and two vestrymen discuss plans for St. James Church, dated 1846 in Dows's label describes an African American sexton, Richard Jenkins, setting off with a pot of A. J. Downing's "tastefully toned buff paint," presumably to touch up the present church edifice. Jenkins may have been free in 1846, but as Hackett says, there was a gallery in that church that was usually occupied by black people.

The most dramatic scene involving slaves in Hyde Park is a night scene set in 1810, where Dr. Samuel Bard gives first aid to William, a negro who has been burnt, with the fire still blazing in the background (Pl. XII). Bard's son holds a lantern, while his son-in-law John McVickar, rector of St. James Church, supports the wounded man and a negro woman sits on the ground nearby with her head bowed. The label notes that McVickar was the first professor of political philosophy (economics) at Kings College (Columbia). Presumably the black man and woman were the slave couple McVickar purchased for a period of seven years, according to his son's biography. McVickar's son writes that he often heard his father say "that slavery, beside its inherent evils, had a most injurious effect on the master, adding always, 'I know it from experience.'"[57] Perhaps this helps account for the solicitude shown the injured slave in this instance.

Olin Dows, mural, 1846—Sexton Richard Jenkins carries a pot of A. J. Downing's special blend of buff paint.

The Story of FDR

The New Deal murals in the Hyde Park post office are to a large extent the story of FDR. Roosevelt himself appears three times in the Hyde Park murals. He is first seen as a young man in 1905 clearing out dead wood with his neighbor Colonel Archibald Rogers to prepare for scientific reforestation. Here we have a prototype for the New Deal program he set such a store by: the Civilian Conservation Corps. He is shown again in 1939 playing host to the king and queen of England at Top Cottage, a famous occasion at which their royal highnesses had the opportunity to sample American hot dogs. The last scene in the series has FDR leaning out of his open automobile going over plans with the school board for the proposed Franklin D. Roosevelt High School, while Fala sits quietly beside the car surveying the chickens in the barnyard. Here we see Roosevelt the architect, the Roosevelt who had asked Stanley-Brown to furnish him a blueprint of a longitudinal section of the

Olin Dows, murals, from top:

1905—Young Franklin D. Roosevelt and Colonel Archibald Rogers clear out dead wood to prepare for scientific reforestation.

(Franklin D. Roosevelt Library)

Picnic at Top Cottage for the King and Queen of England, June 11, 1939.

The President and the Hyde Park School Board discuss plans for the Franklin D. Roosevelt High School, while Fala sits patiently beside the car.

1850—James Roosevelt in his breaking cart at the Union Corners Race Track. Martin Van Buren and his former Secretary of the Navy, James K. Paulding, observe the racing from behind a fence.

54   *THE STAMP OF FDR*

Rhinebeck post office a short time before. FDR intended the new high school and two other new schools in Hyde Park to be understood in a larger political context. He stated at their dedication that they symbolize public works. . .built for the well-being of America.[58]

The president is implied, but not seen, in the view of his iceboat, and in the view of the Mid-Hudson Bridge in the distance, which Dows's label states was dedicated in 1930 by Governor Roosevelt. In a section of "Later Buildings" in the richly-filled sturgeon fishing scene, one sees the "Franklin Delano Roosevelt Library (1940)." He might even be implied, along with his father, in an image of St. James Episcopal Church, where they both served as senior wardens.

Roosevelt's family is pictured in the murals as well. John Roosevelt in the iceboat scene is FDR's uncle. His father, James Roosevelt, talks to a friend from his breaking cart at the Union Corners Race Track in 1850. His mother is on the porch with the president at the famous royal picnic. Mrs. James Roosevelt is mentioned by name in the text listing eight persons seated at two tables with the king and queen. She is implied in the view of the James Roosevelt Memorial Library, as is her husband, since she founded the library in his memory in 1926. Eleanor Roosevelt is shown seated at a third table on the porch at Top Cottage, with her back to the viewer. She is not identified by name in the wall text.

"Springwood" in the Beacon murals and Isaac Roosevelt and the Mid-Hudson Bridge in Poughkeepsie's allude to FDR, but nowhere is his story more evident than in the murals in Hyde Park. He is implied, but not visible, in a small mural of the dedication in the Rhinebeck post office lobby. However, the Hyde Park murals represent the only time that images of Franklin Delano Roosevelt appear in any New Deal post office mural anywhere in the United States.

The trowel Roosevelt used to help lay the building's cornerstone, on display in the lobby today, is a touching symbol of the deepest concerns of this president of the United States of America whose home was in Hyde Park (figs. 63 & 64) The historic implement is engraved: "This trowel was used by Franklin Delano Roosevelt President of the United States of America at the laying of the cornerstone of the United States Agricultural and Post Office Building Wednesday, November 6th, 1940 Twelve O'Clock Noon Hyde Park, New York Presented to the President by Rafferty-Kennedy Co." He laid the cornerstone just twelve hours after his re-election for an unprecedented third term.

Cornerstone, Hyde Park Post Office, 1940, and the trowel used by FDR to lay the cornerstone on display in the lobby.

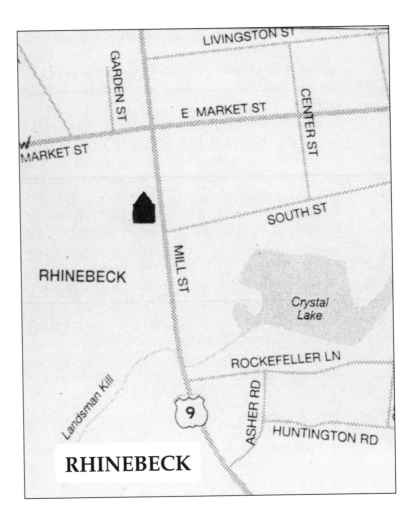

RHINEBECK

Rhinebeck Post Office located
at 14 Mill Street.

THE STAMP OF FDR

Plate I Lobby of the Beacon Post Office

Plate IIa (*above*) Charles Rosen, "Ferry Crossing from Beacon to Newburgh"

Plate IIb (*left*) Charles Rosen, "Old Swedish Church in Beacon"

Plate IIIa Henry Billings, "First Mill on Wappinger Creek, 1780"

Plate IIIb Olin Dows, "Henry Billings Sketching in Rhinebeck Mural"

Plate IV Poughkeepsie Post Office

Plate Va Gerald Foster, Isaac Roosevelt in
Ratification Scene, Poughkeepsie

Plate Vb Gilbert Stuart Portrait of Isaac Roosevelt
at Springwood

Plate VI Gerald Foster, "Hamlet of Poughkeepsie c. 1750"

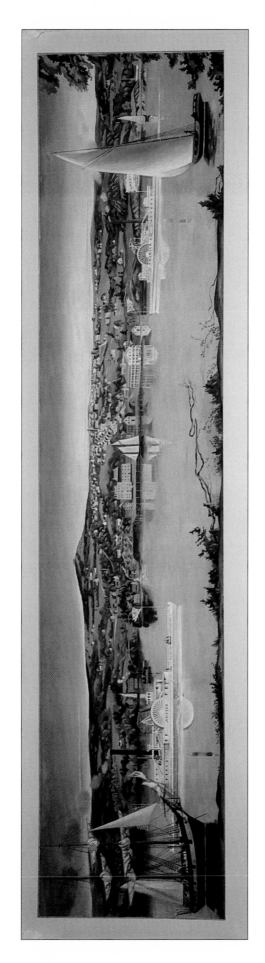

Plate VII Georgina Klitgaard,
"View of the Village of
Poughkeepsie in 1839"

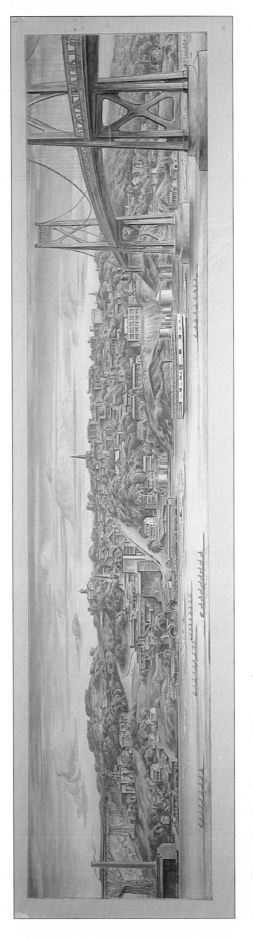

Plate VIII Charles Rosen, "View of the City of Poughkeepsie c. 1939"

Plate IX Hyde Park Post Office

Plate Xa Olin Dows, Indians & *Half Moon* at Anchor, Hyde Park

Plate Xb Olin Dows, Comparable Scene in Rhinebeck

Plate XI Olin Dows, Mending Shad Nets in Hyde Park

Plate XII Olin Dows, Drs. Bard and McVickar Tending Slave Injured in Fire, Hyde Park

Plate XIII Rudolph Stanley-Brown, pencil and ink, Rhinebeck Post Office, gift for FDR (Franklin D. Roosevelt Library)

Plate XIVa Olin Dows, Forest Scene with "Wild Man" Petroglyph

Plate XIVb "Wilderstein," Home of Miss Daisy Suckley (Courtesy of Wilderstein Preservation)

Plate XVa Olin Dows, Slave Making Bricks in a Kiln, Rhinebeck
Plate XVb Olin Dows, Black Youth Husking Corn, Rhinebeck
Plate XVc Olin Dows, Slaves Loading Ship, Rhinebeck

Plate XVI Louis Bouché, "Establishment of First Post Office in Ellenville in 1823"

Rhinebeck:
A Picturesque Post Office

Continue north about eight miles on the Albany Post Road (Route 9) to arrive in the village of Rhinebeck with its 1939 fieldstone post office set back on the left beside the famous Beekman Arms, thought to be the oldest inn in America. Rhinebeck's post office is the most picturesque of the six Dutch Colonial revival post offices in the Mid-Hudson Valley, primarily because of its unusual gabled roof. The curved roof with its asphalt shingles simulating wood and its clipped gable ends sweeps down to form a covered porch all across the front of the building. In his election eve remarks in Rhinebeck in 1940, FDR called Rhinebeck's New Deal post office "one of the best looking post offices in all of the forty-eight states."[59] Many would agree with FDR sixty years later.

The President's Instructions

President Roosevelt called a meeting at the White House in November 1937 at which he gave Admiral Peoples, director of procurement, and Rudolph Stanley-Brown, architect, exact instructions on the design of the post office.[60] The president was especially interested in the building's exterior. The architecture was to replicate one of Rhinebeck's earliest Dutch stone houses, the Kip house, circa 1700. The next owners were Roosevelt ancestors, the Beekmans, who enlarged the house in the eighteenth century. Roosevelt only wanted the original portion of the house duplicated. He was attentive to details, asking that the windows be like their prototypes, with the result that some are sixteen panes over sixteen with wooden sashes. He wished the little bull's eye window on the upper story to be repeated, believing it to have been a means of defense against Indian attacks. He was willing to approve one minor exterior change: the porch roof could curve and extend across the entire front (Pl. XIII).

Cornerstone, Rhinebeck Post Office, 1939, and model of the Kip-Beekman House, inspiration for the Rhinebeck Post Office.

(The Museum of Rhinebeck History)

The model for the post office burned in 1910. Rudolph Stanley-Brown was empowered to negotiate the sale of stones from the ruins of the eighteenth-century house for the post office replica. This was a unique opportunity among all of the Mid-Hudson group mandated to use local fieldstone. Roosevelt wanted it to be recorded in an inscription that the stone came from the Beekman house.[61] A stone slab embedded in the porch wall at the far right reads: "This Building (Except the rear) is a replica of the exterior of that part of the Beekman House constructed near Rhinebeck in AD 1700 by Henrick Kip Stone from the original structure has been used in the construction of this building." In addition, two artifacts salvaged from the Beekman house are on display in the lobby in wall cases Stanley-Brown designed expressly for this purpose. One is a stone lintel from an opening in the old Beekman house on which the house's date, "1700," is carved. The other is a pane of glass scratched with the initials of Margaret Beekman, rescued from the fire in 1910 by John Jacob Astor.

Rudolph Stanley-Brown's wife, Katherine, tells a delightful story in her unpublished journal regarding their visit to the house that was to serve as the model:

Rudy and I, flanked on the back seat by two Secret Service men, the president driving his manual-controlled

THE STAMP OF FDR

car, set out from his mother's house in Hyde Park where we were staying to see the old Beekman house. It had windows the president was duplicating in an upcoming county building. Rudy had been boning up on Dutchess County colonial architecture and remarked that he thought that muntins in the windows would be about three-quarters of an inch wide. FDR said, 'I think you'll find, my boy, they're exactly one inch across.' It was embarrassing when we arrived at the house to find that the president's answer was absolutely accurate. Embarrassing, that is, if the president had not added as an afterword: 'That's the kind of thing I remember. Not particularly useful in politics but absorbing to me.' No wonder we all adored him.[62]

Roosevelt did care that the public areas inside the building mirror the look of an early eighteenth-century interior. In Rhinebeck, the look extends to the postmaster's private office which has paneled walls simulating an eighteenth-century parlor. The lobby has similarly-paneled pine wainscotting and trim, and a hand-hewn beamed ceiling, serving to set off Olin Dows's murals to advantage. FDR had wanted four large paintings framed in the Dutch style of 1700 as lobby decoration, but he was persuaded to accept a painted frieze instead. Other period details—a random width, pegged oak floor, and a split Dutch door with wrought strap hinges and rosehead nails, help create the proper ambience. At the same time, the architect added a contemporary touch in the stylized bronze grilles of repeated geometric patterns calling to mind rows of flowers. The juxtaposition of historicism and modernism in this post office interior is reminiscent of Kebbon's pairing of the old and the new in the post office lobby in Poughkeepsie.

The lobby in *Murals in the Rhinebeck Post Office* with modern-style ventilation grilles and murals by Olin Dows.

Margaret L. Suckley, known as "Daisy," played a considerable role in the formation of the Rhinebeck post office. She was eminently suited to do so. Like the artist, Olin Dows, she was a Rhinebeck native and a descendant of both Beekmans and Livingstons. She, too, was a member of a River family that socialized with the Roosevelts and a distant cousin of FDR. Daisy Suckley and the president were sixth cousins. Their relationship went beyond any obvious connections. After her death in 1991, correspondence between them and notes in her diaries revealed what Geoffrey Ward calls "an intimate friendship."[63] Traces of that intimate friendship are left in the final Hyde Park mural showing FDR's little dog, Fala, which she gave him and which he dearly loved (pictured beside the president on page 54).

Daisy Suckley helped FDR strategize getting the site he wanted beside the Beekman Arms, which involved tearing down the old Town Hall. Roosevelt believed it would be no great architectural loss, as the 1879 red-brick Victorian building was "not in good taste." Some townspeople did not agree. Suckley advised the president by letter that the Post Office Department should take up the subject directly with the Town Board, suggesting which members to approach and which to avoid. "Also, it would be best not to mention the Beekman house or anything *to do* with the type of building, until the site is settled by a special election."[64] The Beekman house ruins were on Suckley family property, but her brother Arthur and her sister Katherine were the legal owners. Stanley-Brown visited Arthur Suckley armed with advice from his sister Daisy as to what kind of agreement to suggest to procure the stone for the post office. One condition she proposed which was unac-

Daisy Suckley cruising the Hudson River on the presidential yacht, *USS Potomac*, September 1937.

(Franklin D. Roosevelt Library)

ceptable to her brother, was that the stone be donated to the government. He wished to be paid and agreed to the sum of fifty cents per cubic yard. Daisy Suckley had the stone lintel and the glass pane from the Beekman house in her possession. She lent them to the post office, asking only that they not be incorporated into the outside of the building, but rather to be kept inside for better protection. Olin Dows is credited with persuading FDR to change his mind to allow murals on the post office walls instead of Dutch-style paintings. However, another persuasive voice has recently been heard. In a letter in November 1937, Daisy Suckley wrote: "Dear Franklin. . . . I've been wondering if, after all, it might not be interesting to have historical murals in the P.O. because, no matter what the architecture may be *outside*, the *inside* will be a modern P.O. Aff–D."[65] It is hard to disentangle an interlocking network of friends and relations with common objectives, but it seems fairly certain that a gentle suggestion from Roosevelt's special friend and neighbor in 1937 had an effect on how the Rhinebeck lobby was decorated.

There is an emblematic reference in the murals to Daisy Suckley's home in Rhinebeck. The reference is through a depiction of the so-called Indian stone in the foreground of the first panel (Pl. XIVa). The Indian stone, bearing what some assume to be a petroglyph of a "wild man," is appropriate in its early eighteenth-century setting. When Daisy Suckley's father acquired a river front site in the nineteenth century and built a house upon it, he named his estate "Wilderstein," (wild man's stone) in reference to the nearby petroglyph. The Indian stone in the Rhinebeck murals points directly to the Suckley estate where both FDR and Olin Dows frequently came to call (Pl. XIVb).

Murals in the Rhinebeck Post Office

The Civic Club of Rhinebeck published a handsome booklet in 1940, *Murals in the Rhinebeck Post Office*, with Olin Dows's watercolor sketches of the post office murals accompanied by his explanatory notes.[66] The notes match the wall text for the twelve connected panels in the lobby. The Rhinebeck murals illustrate the history and life of that community in a similar fashion to Dows's murals in Hyde Park. Although the friezes have the same starting point–the arrival of Henry Hudson's *Half Moon* observed by Native Americans in the woods–they diverge by focusing on the eighteenth century in Rhinebeck and on the nineteenth century in Hyde Park, before leaping forward to the present (Pl. X). It is probably not totally coincidental, as Rhoads says, that FDR's ancestors were in Rhinebeck in the eighteenth century, while his family only moved to Hyde Park when his father bought a house there in 1867.[67]

Dows observes in the text for the first panel that "Native wild life and vegetation, as well as many actual views, run through these murals." The artist began this practice with his first mural when he was twenty: an overall pattern of white owls amid climbing vines in the nearby River estate, Callender House. It is interesting to observe a comparable owl peering out from a hole in a tree above the Indian stone many years later in Rhinebeck. Another sign of this artist, once removed, is the conspicuous image of his sister Deborah Dows's Great Dane stretched out comfortably beside his friend Henry Billings, while he sketches (See Pl. III). Dows's signature appears on an upturned apple crate in the orchard scene farther on.

Signs of Slavery in Rhinebeck

There are pictorial signs of slavery in Rhinebeck, but these are not mentioned in the texts. In a section dated 1774, an African American man kneels to tend a homemade kiln where bricks are baked, while a white man lays bricks with mortar from a scaffolding (Pl. XVa). A black youth bends to pick up husks at a festive cornhusking bee in 1780 (Pl. XVb). In a busy river scene dated 1807, several male slaves lean to carry heavy sacks onto a ship from a dock (Pl. XVc). In Rhinebeck as in Hyde Park, slaves are pictured doing hard labor that allowed the community to prosper. In an early version of the text for the 1807 panel, Dows did refer to "slaves. . .loading a sloop with grain," but the passage was dropped from the final version.[68] The question of why slaves were pictured several times but never identified as such in the Rhinebeck murals is difficult to answer.

FDR and Family in the Rhinebeck Murals

FDR is indicated once in the Rhinebeck murals, dedicating the post office on May 1, 1939. Members of his family are seated on the porch for the ceremony, but it is hard to distinguish them or the president in the small mural above the exit. A frieze that culminates in a scene with President Roosevelt involved in some New Deal architectural project he helped to instigate is comparable to Dows's Hyde Park frieze that ends in a similar manner, with the president surveying plans for a federally-funded high school.

FDR is indicated by extension in the murals whenever his ancestors are depicted. This would be the case when his Beekman ancestors are shown and described as early settlers of Rhinebeck. Roosevelt made the Beekman connec-

tion explicit when he spoke at the post office dedication. He spoke then also of his great-great-grandfather Isaac Roosevelt, saying he "lived in Rhinebeck for some time during the revolution and was a member of the Dutchess county militia."[69] This is the same Isaac Roosevelt who appears prominently in another capacity in the Poughkeepsie murals. Here he is shown and cited in the text as among the congregation of the Dutch Reformed Church. Thus Roosevelt's Dutch ancestry is confirmed. One of FDR's living relatives, a first cousin who resided in Rhinebeck, is mentioned in the text pertaining to "some outstanding Rhinebeck buildings." A mid-nineteenth-century building is "now the Woman's Exchange, where food and clothing made locally are sold under the direction of Miss Laura Delano."

Roosevelt could be implied in a scene of apple pickers sitting in a group listening to "radio news." FDR was the first president to address the nation by radio. By 1941, radio talks became his hallmark. After his first radio address in 1933, his fellow historian and consultant for the Rhinebeck murals Helen Wilkinson Reynolds wrote to FDR asking how he managed to be so effective in explaining the banking crisis to the American people. Roosevelt replied that he sat at his desk in the White House and tried to visualize three types of people representative of the overwhelming majority. One type he pictured was a farmer in his field, a "kind of individual citizen he had known so well in Dutchess County all my life."[70] These Dutchess County farmers listening to radio news in Rhinebeck seem to visualize what Roosevelt told Miss Reynolds he conjured up in his imagination when he spoke to the American people.

TOP: Olin Dows, mural, Contemporary scene of a group of apple pickers listening to radio news.

ABOVE: FDR delivers a nationwide radio address, a "Fireside Chat," ca. 1938.
(Franklin D. Roosevelt Library)

TOP: Crowd scene at the
Rhinebeck Post Office Dedication.

(Franklin D. Roosevelt Library)

ABOVE: Program for the dedication of the Rhinebeck Post
Office.

"The Most Thoroughly Dedicated Small-Town Post Office in the Western Hemisphere"

In his foreword to *Murals in the Rhinebeck Post Office*,
William Seabrook quotes the statement that Rhinebeck was
"without doubt the most thoroughly dedicated small-town
post office in the Western Hemisphere." The dedication fes-
tivities began with a parade led by a marshal and mounted
state troopers, color guards and marching bands, and
"Danish Girls–Scandinavian-American Society," the latter
because of the unusual presence of the crown prince and
princess of Denmark and Iceland. The ceremony on the
post office porch opened with an invocation, after which
the Honorable Henry Morgenthau Jr., secretary of the
Treasury presented the new post office to the Honorable
James A. Farley, postmaster general. The president of the
United States then gave the dedication address that ended
with his turning over a trowel to his royal highness Crown
Prince Frederik of Denmark and Iceland, to lay the cornerstone. A selection by the Eighteenth infantry band and a
benediction concluded the ceremony. The momentous
occasion involving European royalty and the president of
the United States of America was summed up on a bronze

tablet installed on the wall in the post office lobby. In addition to the post office ceremony, the program noted that there would be another event later in the day at the old Dutch church. Frank D. Blanchard, minister, would deliver an address by Henry Beekman's grave and memorial tablets of the Beekman and Livingston families: "The Tradition of Beekman House."

The dedication of the Rhinebeck post office drew crowds of spectators to see the Danish royalty, as well as to witness the ceremonies. The dedication also attracted a large amount of media coverage, including radio and news reels and an army of metropolitan reporters and photographers. Margaret Bourke-White was among them. Rhinebeck might also have had the most thoroughly *recorded* small-town post office dedication in the Western Hemisphere. To what was recorded that day might be added two records after the fact: the painted scene of the dedication and the bronze tablet commemorating the event on the lobby walls.

TOP: FDR speaking at the Rhinebeck dedication, with Secretary of the Treasury Morgenthau, Postmaster General Farley, and illustrious guests, the Crown Prince and Princess of Denmark and Iceland, in attendance.
(Franklin D. Roosevelt Library)

ABOVE: Bronze dedication plaque in the post office lobby, noting that the cornerstone was laid by Crown Prince Frederik of Denmark and Iceland.

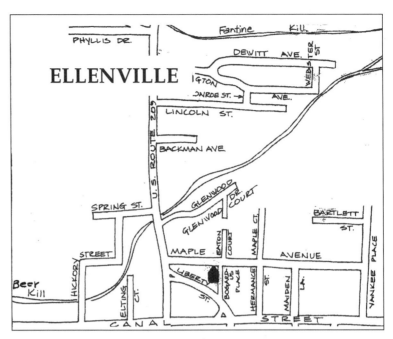

Ellenville Post Office on Liberty Place and its corner-stone, 1940

THE STAMP OF FDR

Ellenville:
FDR'S Stamp on Ulster

SOME TWENTY MILES west of the Hudson River and due west of Hyde Park and Poughkeepsie is Ellenville in Ulster County, which has the only post office in the group outside of Dutchess County. Ulster County purportedly came next in FDR's affections after Dutchess County because of ancestral ties and its proximity to Hyde Park.[71] He had hoped to attend a dedication, but events in Europe forced him to stay in Washington. The post office opened without fanfare on October 15, 1940.

Ellenville's fieldstone post office barely escaped being brick. The contract for such construction was close to being let when some Ellenville citizens, who had seen pictures of Rhinebeck's new post office in the newspapers, decided they wanted a comparable building. Tuthill McDowell the postmaster, who was also the town chairman, sent FDR a letter via Franklin Wilson, the rector of St. James Church in Hyde Park, and his wife, noting that Mrs. Wilson and her family had been neighbors in Ellenville for years. The politically astute gentleman also pointed out that the site selected for the post office is on the corner of a square between the Wayside Inn, a hotel where a banquet was given in Roosevelt's honor when he was governor of New York State, and another building where McDowell's mother had escorted Mrs. Roosevelt to meet with a group of Ellenville ladies.[72] When the letter got no immediate response, McDowell and two civic leaders sent FDR a telegram, which did goad him into action. As the president told Mr. Wilson, "I will stop that brick right away!"[73] A more restrained letter to the town chairman from the White House stated, "I have requested the architects of the Treasury Department to redesign the facade of the Ellenville Post Office in keeping with the traditional architecture of Rondout Valley, and making use of native stone."[74] Because of FDR's dramatic intervention, as well as for reasons shared with others in the group, it is apt to call

Ellenville's New Deal post office "FDR's Stamp on Ulster," as an Ellenville newspaper once did.

Architect Rudolph Stanley-Brown duly toured the Rondout Valley from Kingston to Ellenville seeking out and photographing early Dutch Colonial structures that might serve as a model for the post office building. It is quite possible that the design was based, to some extent, on the then extant Johannes G. Hardenberg House, a 1762 stone farmhouse pictured and described in Helen Wilkinson Reynolds's book on pre-revolutionary Dutch houses in the Hudson Valley for which Roosevelt wrote the introduction. The historic Hardenberg House which McDowell had put forth in his letter to the president as a possible model for the new post office had been the repository for state documents when the British burned Kingston, the first state capital, during the Revolutionary War.[75] In any event, the sturdy one-story post office reflects a characteristic eighteenth-century Ulster County stone house, with stones quarried from nearby Accord. The roof's asphalt shingles simulate wooden ones from colonial days. Clapboard covers the top portions of the gabled ends of the one-and-a-half-story building pierced by sash windows. The clapboard finish corresponds to the entablature of the small gabled porch at the entrance. The porch is reached by bluestone steps with wrought-iron railings, and by the modern addition of a wheelchair ramp. In contrast to his three other New Deal post offices, which make reference to Dutch Colonial domestic architecture, Stanley-Brown chose to embellish this one with a square cupola with bell and hanging rope topped by a narrow spire and a pierced iron weather vane in the shape of an arrow. It seems appropriate that the federal building that takes its cue from revolutionary times faces onto Liberty Place. The bell in the tower

Ellenville's distinctive square cupola with bell topped with fleche and pierced weather vane.

Ellenville lobby looking towards Louis Bouché's mural, 1942, "Establishment of the First Post Office in Ellenville."

was rung on July 4, 1976, in tribute to America's Declaration of Independence.[76]

The L-shaped lobby has a flagstone floor and wooden wainscotting eight feet high in imitation of eighteenth-century paneling. The glassed-in entryway and the windows' deep reveals have matching paneling. Both utilize hand-drawn glass lights or panes with noticeable imperfections that enhance the period feeling of the lobby. The glass panes and the paneling, along with wooden customer tables with scalloped aprons and turned legs, create a warm vintage ambience for a modern, up-to-date post office.

"Louis Bouché 1942"

The Rhinebeck post office comes into play again in regard to Ellenville's mural. An Ellenville citizen, Deyo W. Johnson, had read a favorable newspaper report of Olin Dows's sketches of his Rhinebeck murals exhibited at the Art Students League in New York. He wrote to ask Dows how to get murals for Ellenville's post office, and if he would be willing to do them. Dows promptly replied that he would not be available, but that there were many fine painters in competition for the Poughkeepsie post office whom he thought were due jobs in this locality. He suggested Johnson pursue the matter with Edward Bruce, chief of the Section of Fine Arts. Dows sent Bruce a copy of his letter, and another one suggesting Judson Smith or some other Woodstock artist who had submitted good sketches for Poughkeepsie. Dows added that as he remembered, Stanley-Brown was doing the post office so that he will make a good place for it.[77]

On January 21, 1941, the assistant chief of the Section Edward Rowan invited Louis Bouché to submit designs for a mural decoration in Ellenville.[78] Louis Bouché (1896-1969) was an accomplished painter who received his artistic training in Paris and New York. He was a Guggenheim Fellow in 1933. He won several important mural commissions, including ones at the Interior and Justice Depart-

Judson Smith's sketch for the competition for a Poughkeepsie mural, about 1935. Smith was suggested as a possible artist for Ellenville.
The Frances Lehman Loeb Art Center, Vassar College, Gift of the Judson Smith Family

THE STAMP OF FDR

ments in Washington and at Radio City Music Hall. He went on to teach at the National Academy of Design. Bouché's designs for the Ellenville post office did meet with approval, and he was paid $1,000 for the finished work. He signed his mural in the left-hand corner: "Louis Bouché 1942."

Establishment of First Post Office in Ellenville in 1823

Bouché's oil canvas five foot seven inches by thirteen foot ten inches, covers the lobby's northwest wall above the wainscotting (Pl. XVI). It is a jubilant painting celebrating the establishment of Ellenville's own post office in 1823. The scene centers on a log building, a general store, owned by Charles Hartshorne, where the first post office was

"Louis Bouché 1937," photograph of self portrait.
(Woodstock Artists Association Archives)

located. A group of men had met at the store and agreed to ask the federal government for a post office, but they had trouble agreeing on a name for what had simply been called "The City." Finally, Hartshorne was dispatched to ask the ladies for a suggestion. The painting captures the moment a cry goes up when Hartshorne returns and reports on his success in securing a new name: Ellenville. The source of the name was Ellen Snyder, a visitor at the home of Nathan Hoornbeek who lived nearby. She said, "Name it after me, call it Ellenville," and they did, thus paving the way for a post office.

An Enlightening Correspondence

An ongoing correspondence between Bouché and Edward Rowan as the project progressed reveals the enormous amount of care the artist put into creating this mural. Moreover, it reads like a case study of what the Section required of its artists. Where possible, the artist should visit the town where the mural was to be located and consult with the postmaster and leading citizens about the choice of subject matter. If a visit was not feasible, the artist was to write to the postmaster for advice and do library research at home. The Section called this its "universal plan."[79]

Bouché visited the Ellenville post office in early April 1941 and discussed the subject matter with the postmaster and another official. The postmaster lent him a history of Ulster County where he read of the naming of the village in 1823. He asked the postmaster to dig up more history for him if possible from some of the old residents. At the same time, the artist began a search of old prints of the locality and of this approximate period. He told Rowan that he went through everything in the New York Public Library and the New-York Historical Society, and he had written to the Ulster County Historical Society in Kingston. He reported to Rowan the subject matter he had decided upon, and his plan to use some of the likenesses of the present Ellenville post office staff for the famous meeting. They liked the idea, he said; as a matter of fact, it was their idea.

Bouché wrote that since he had been unable to find any prints of the place in the 1800s, he went back to Ellenville in late April to do some landscape sketching so that at least the mountain background would have some accuracy. He stood on top of various buildings to get an unimpeded view. He also found a local photographer to take pictures for him to work from in New York. Bouché sent Rowan a colored sketch on June 10, with a letter saying he would study the costumes carefully in his cartoon. One evidence that he did so comes from a young man in the scene resplendently dressed in a U.S. Army uniform. However, the uniform is the artist's interpretation of an army uniform in the 1820s, taken from H. A. Ogden's popular *History of Uniforms* (1888). It is not actually accurate for the time.[80]

By November 29, 1941, Bouché was able to write to Rowan that he was terribly eager to get going on the painting and he hoped it wouldn't be necessary for him to keep his cartoon and sketch too long. "I have every hope that the mural will look swell in place." In the end, Bouché thought the Ellenville mural was better than either the Interior or Justice jobs. In fact, he thought it was better than any mural he had ever done. Tuthill McDowell missed seeing Bouché in May when he came up from New York for the installation. He wrote the artist of his intense satisfaction, saying it fit perfectly with the style of building we have. Everyone admires it, McDowell said, which very much surprised him. People usually find fault with something done by a stranger.

The final step was to send Rowan a small colored sketch incorporating all last minute changes to the mural to present to FDR. Bouché sent it off on August 12, 1943, with a note saying: "I hope I am not too late for the honor of having it hung in the White House."

A Complete History of the Post Office in Ellenville

The Ellenville mural and the new post office building span the entire history of the Ellenville post office. Together they serve as a visual record of the history of that post office from the beginning in 1823 up until 1942. A Poughkeepsie mural pictures its New Deal post office in a cityscape, and Rhinebeck does this in a dedication scene. But neither encompasses local post office history as completely as Ellenville, where art and architecture work in combination.

THIS REMARKABLE GROUP of New Deal post offices situated in Beacon, Wappingers Falls, Poughkeepsie, Hyde Park, Rhinebeck, and Ellenville—each with its own story and each part of a larger story of the role of FDR–has a good deal to tell us. These post offices in relatively small communities remind us to look beyond major cities when searching for significant architecture in the New Deal era. The murals caution us to look outside museum walls for notable American painting in the same time period.

Roosevelt himself called attention to the value of art in New Deal post offices in his speech at the dedication of the National Gallery of Art in Washington on March 17, 1941. The president was there to accept Andrew Mellon's gift of the building and an art collection, along with other important art collections, "for the people of the United States." Roosevelt noted that in the past, for most Americans, "art was something foreign to America and to themselves." However, he said, "recently. . .they have discovered that they have a part. They have seen in their own towns, in their own villages, in school houses, in post offices. . .pictures by their sons and neighbors. . .all of it native, human, eager, and alive–all of it painted about things they know and look at often and have touched and loved." He obviously saw no fast line between his administration's gift of

Roosevelt speaking at the dedication of the National Gallery of Art in Washington, D. C., March 15, 1941

(National Gallery of Art Archives)

THE STAMP OF FDR

art in more ordinary public places and the gift of a museum filled with old master paintings for the public's enjoyment and edification, free of charge.

"FDR as Architect," a self-styled identity which Roosevelt assumed and which others recognized sixty years ago, is manifested in this group of post offices. The post offices indicate a further identity, "FDR as Civic Planner." His concern for civic planning becomes apparent in his recommendation for the placement of the post offices, and his desire to have buildings work in concert to create a handsome public space. Even though his first plan for Wappingers Falls was thwarted, the post office as sited helped form a larger park-like ensemble. The post office in Hyde Park extended to the corner by its landscaped lot with its vintage stone well created another appealing public space. Roosevelt came close to realizing a genuine civic plaza in Poughkeepsie. In his speech at the Rhinebeck dedication, he went so far as to suggest that in the future, Victorian buildings too close to the street should be replaced by a Colonial type set back to create "a large open square admired for its beauty by all who pass." The president's interest in city planning was evident as late as 1944, when he sent his principal post office architect, Rudolph Stanley-Brown, to Augusta, Georgia, to make a future plan for that city. The architect died of a fever contracted there in the process.

The Dutch Colonial revival buildings modeled on buildings of the past, using comparable construction methods and materials, increase our knowledge and understanding of another era, as do the scenes of local history inside. Post offices as copies of previous buildings, employing re-used "spolia" in the form of historic stones collected near at hand, demonstrate an unusual method of historic preservation practiced by the president of the United States. The art and architecture and the reused materials together indicate a strong need to record, and to record publicly in a manner that will endure. This is "FDR the Historian" at work in a special way, something which such tangible evidence as engraved trowels, inscribed cornerstones, plus an extra explanatory cornerstone in Rhinebeck, and bronze tablets clearly reflects.

We see how the historic paintings and historic architecture were put to another purpose, by pointing to selected highlights of the past that would give hope by example for better times to come. In so doing, they illustrate what the head of the WPA Federal Art Project Holger Cahill called "a usable past," a concept President Roosevelt espoused. The usable past in this instance extends to implicit support for the president's political activities in the present. The post offices teach us what is already known in other ways: FDR is a consummate politician. Secretary of the Treasury Morgenthau's concluding words at the dedication of the Poughkeepsie post office in 1937 were that the structure "will always recall the interest of Franklin Roosevelt in American architecture and in that sense will be a monument to him."[81] The six post offices in aggregate actually comprise a larger, richer monument, FDR's monument to himself, which continues to live on, as he had intended.

Finally, the post offices reveal a consistency about the interests of FDR and the way they intertwine. Preservation and the postal service came together when he was governor of New York and had milestone markers on the Albany Post Road protected by stone enclosures. As a boy, he inherited a stamp collection from his uncle that launched him on a lifetime avocation. As president, Roosevelt personally approved the design of each of more than two hundred stamps issued during his twelve years in office. During that time, he made suggestions for some and rejected others. He took full credit for one design himself, the six

The Newburgh Peace stamp issued April 19, 1933; sheet signed "Franklin D. Roosevelt" and "Henry Morgenthau Jr."

(Franklin D. Roosevelt Library)

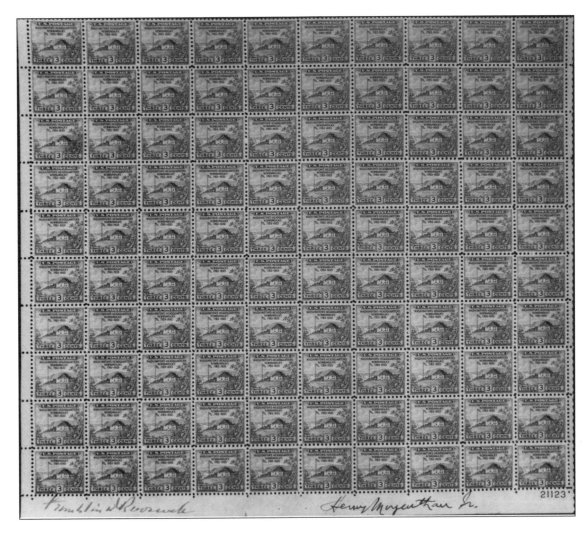

THE STAMP OF FDR

cent airmail stamp of 1938, and partial credit for others. Thus Roosevelt's interest in design manifested in post office architecture found an additional outlet in a related subject, postal stamps.

The Most Meaningful Stamp to FDR

Five days after his inauguration as president on March 4, 1933, Roosevelt asked Postmaster General James A. Farley to proceed with the issuance of a stamp requested during Hoover's administration by Representative Hamilton Fish of Orange County, New York. This was the Newburgh Peace issue, commemorating George Washington's Proclamation of Peace ending the Revolutionary War in 1783. The stamp depicts a stone Dutch farmhouse in Newburgh built by Jonathan Hasbrouck in 1770 where Washington had his headquarters when he issued his proclamation. In selecting from the die proofs, Roosevelt picked the one that showed the Hudson River to the left of the house in the central design. An image of the same Dutch stone farmhouse labeled "Washington's Headquarters-NEWBURGH" appears in Rosen's view of the Hudson in the Beacon post office four years later (Pl. IIa).

The philatelist Brian Baur calls the Newburgh Peace stamp the most meaningful to FDR of all the stamps issued during his administration. Roosevelt told Postmaster Farley that the Newburgh commemorative stamp had the greatest personal historic interest for him.[82] It is not surprising that someone who cared about his political identity and his historic office first held by George Washington, who loved the Hudson River Valley and its history so much, and who felt deeply about Dutch Colonial architecture, should declare the Newburgh commemorative stamp to have the greatest personal historic interest. An addition-

Conclusion

al reason might be that Roosevelt's Dutch ancestry was traceable to Newburgh through his mother's family.[83] The little postage stamp sums up much of what there is to learn about Franklin D. Roosevelt through surveying the post offices in the Mid-Hudson Valley to which he gave his devoted attention from the White House.

THE STAMP OF FDR

Notes

1. Jeff Muise, "FDR's Stamp on Ulster," *Ellenville Journal*, undated clipping, MVF-Ellenville Post Office, Ellenville Public Library and Museum.

2. William B. Rhoads, "Franklin D. Roosevelt and Dutch Colonial Architecture," *New York History* LIX (October 1978): 430–464, p. 463f.

3. Ibid.

4. Harlan Althen, "F. D. R. As Architect," *New York Times Magazine*, December 8, 1940, pp. 9 and 26.

5. John C. Ferris, "Franklin D. Roosevelt: His Development and Accomplishments as a Local Historian," *Dutchess County Historical Society Year Book* 68 (1983): 16–39.

6. Helen Wilkinson Reynolds, *Dutch Houses in the Hudson Valley before 1776*. Introduction by Franklin D. Roosevelt, originally published for the Holland Society by Payson & Clarke in 1929, and reprinted by Dover Publications, Inc., New York, 1965.

7. "Informal Remarks of the President Beacon, N.Y. November 4, 1940," Franklin D. Roosevelt Library.

8. FDR's columns in the *Standard* as well as ones that he wrote for the *Macon Daily Telegraph* are published in Donald Scott Carmichael, ed., with a foreword by Eleanor Roosevelt, *F. D. R. Columnist* (Chicago: Pellegrini & Cudahy, 1947).

9. Morg Hoyt, "Turning Back the Clock," the *Standard*. Hoyt, a delegate to the Democratic State Senatorial Convention in 1910, participated in the decision to use an automobile. I would like to thank Robert Murphy, president of the Beacon Historical Society, for providing me with a copy of Hoyt's column written sometime in the 1950s.

10. National Register of Historic Places Inventory, nomination form, 1980/1985. The Beacon post office along with the rest of the Mid-Hudson group was listed on the National Register in 1988 under: "United States Post Offices in New York State 1858–1943–Thematic Resources."

11. "Morgenthau's Speech at P. O.," *Poughkeepsie Eagle-News*, May 2, 1939, p. 9.

12. NRHP Inventory, nomination form, 1980/1985, Beacon N.Y. post office.

13. Editorial, *Beacon News*, October 14, 1937, p. 4.

14. Note on the reverse of a construction photograph initialed "GSU 7-13-36."

15. Rhoads, "FDR and Colonial Architecture," p. 441.

16. Polly Kline, *The Art Students League in Woodstock* (Woodstock, N.Y.: The Woodstock School of Art, Inc., 1987), n.p.

17. Marlene Park & Gerald E. Markowitz, *New Deal for Art* (Hamilton, N.Y.: Gallery Association of New York State, Inc., 1977), p. 4.

18. William B. Rhoads, "The Artistic Patronage of Franklin D. Roosevelt: Art as Historical Record," *Prologue. Journal of the National Archives* 15 (Spring 1983): 4–21, p. 15, n. 37.

19. "INFORMAL REMARKS OF THE PRESIDENT NEWBURGH, N.Y., November 4, 1940," Franklin Delano Roosevelt Library (FDRL).

20. An interview with Stanley-Brown's daughter, Katherine Stanley-Brown Abbott, 16 April 2000, provided a good deal of personal and written information about this architect. The unpublished journal of her mother, Katherine Oliver Stanley-Brown, furnished a description of the first Sunday night supper.

21. Rhoads, "FDR and Colonial Architecture," pp. 450–452.

22. William B. Rhoads, "Olin Dows, Art, History, and a Usable Past," *The Livingston Legacy*, ed. by Richard T. Wiles (Bard College, 1987): 427–440, p. 431. Billings executed two more post office murals for the Section of Fine Arts in Medford, Mass. and Lake Placid, N.Y. and a 68 foot-wide stage drop for the former Franklin Delano Roosevelt High School in Hyde Park.

23. The marquis's diary quoted in Reynolds, *Dutch Houses Before 1776*, p. 331.

24. Press Conference #599, Vol. 14: 308–309, FDRL.

25. Rhoads, "Artistic Patronage," p. 19.

26. NRHP Inventory, nomination form, 1980/1985, Poughkeepsie, N.Y. post office. Words cast in the metal on the bell read: "This bell was cast by direction of Franklin Delano Roosevelt, thirty-second president of the United States of America ANNO DOMINI MCMXXXVIII 'Ring the perpetuation of American freedom' Meneely & Company, Waterville, New York." The Poughkeepsie post office kindly researched the bell's cost in its inventory records.

27. Merritt C. Speidel and FDR were clearly of one mind. In 1940, Speidel built a new plant in Chillicothe, Ohio, to house his three newspapers there as a fieldstone replica of the first capital of Ohio. One of the historic newspapers, the *Chillicothe Gazette*, was older than the state of Ohio itself. Two stones from the original state house were installed beside the entrance portico, surmounted by bronze plaques, one calling attention to the historical significance of the stones and the other listing the names of the papers, "Famous Newspapers' New Home Replica First Ohio State Capital," *Sunday Courier*, April 28, 1940, pp. 1, 4.

28. "Informal, Extemporaneous Remarks of the President at the Dedication of the New Post Office and in Commemoration of Two Hundred and Fiftieth Anniversary of the Founding of the City of Poughkeepsie, New York, October 13, 1937," p. 2, FDRL, and William B. Rhoads, "Poughkeepsie's Architectural Styles, 1835-1940: Anarchy or Decorum," in Clyde Griffen, ed., *Poughkeepsie's Past: New Perspectives* (Poughkeepsie, N.Y.: Dutchess County Historical Society, 1988):18–55, p. 32.

29. Harold F. Gosnell, *Champion Campaigner* (New York: Macmillan Company, 1952), p. 28. Cited in F. Kennon Moody, "F.D.R.: Neighbors and Politics in Dutchess County," *Transformations of an American County. Dutchess County, New York 1683–1983* (Poughkeepsie, N.Y.: Dutchess County Historical Society, 1986): 87–98, p. 91.

30. "Informal, Extemporaneous Remarks of the President," p. 2, FDRL.

31. William B. Rhoads, "The President and the Sesquicentennial of the Constitution: Franklin Roosevelt's Monument in Poughkeepsie," *New York History* LVII (July 1990):

309–321, p. 321.

32. Ibid, p. 314.

33. Letter dated January 16, 1940, Press Conferences, v. 14, pp. 308–309, FDRL.

34. Rhoads, "The President and the Sesquicentennial," p. 317.

35. Ibid, p. 317, n. 17.

36. Karal Ann Marling, *Wall-to-Wall America. A Cultural History of Post-Office Murals in the Great Depression* (Minneapolis: Univ. of Minnesota Press, 1982), pp. 53–55.

37. Rhoads, "Artistic Patronage of Franklin D. Roosevelt," p. 16 and n. 42.

38. Louise Jonas, "Her Light Came to be a Symbol of courage. Thus Georgina Klitgaard, Creator of Post Office Mural, Became a Legend in Catskill Mountains," *Sunday Poughkeepsie New Yorker*, November 21, 1943, p. 2A.

39. Karal Ann Marling, "A Note on New Deal Iconography: Futurology and the Historical Myth," *Prospects* 4 (1979): 421–440, p. 435. Georgina Klitgaard used similar techniques to similar effect in 1941 in a post office mural in Pelham, Georgia entitled, "Pelham Landscape." There is a timeless quality about the rural landscape centering on a pond framed by branches.

40. Ibid, p. 433.

41. FDRL. A copy of Nixon's letter is on display in the Poughkeepsie post office lobby. The trowel had been in the custody of the Roosevelt Library in Hyde Park.

42. Rhoads, "Roosevelt and Dutch Colonial Architecture," p. 453f.

43. Roosevelt's speech at post office dedication, 6 November 1940, FDRL.

44. "Roosevelt Plans to Inspect Site for Post Office," (Poughkeepsie) *Sunday Courier*, April 7, 1940, p. 2. Following the policy of keeping the public informed, a story describing the proposed building in some detail appeared in the same newspaper on June 16, along with an attractive sketch by Rudolph Stanley-Brown.

45. Rhoads, "Roosevelt and Dutch Colonial Architecture," p. 454f and n. 55.

46. Rhoads, "Olin Dows," p. 429.

47. Olin Dows, "Murals in the Post Offices at Rhinebeck and Hyde Park Dutchess County," *Dutchess County Historical Society Year Book* 27 (1942): 24–28, p. 27.

48. Olin Dows Papers, FDRL.

49. Handwritten note, n.d., FDRL.

50. Letter from R. Stanley-Brown to Mr. Olin Dows, Rhinebeck, New York, December 6, 1940, FDRL. After describing how drawings were made in 1844, Stanley-Brown ended the letter by saying that if "you want to see what those old drawings are like when you are next here we could dig out of the Supervising Architect's files drawings made about that period."

51. Letter from Olin Dows to Rudolph Stanley-Brown, December 10, 1940, FDRL.

52. Typed transcript of *"MY DAY* BY ELEANOR ROOSEVELT," copyright 1941, Eleanor Roosevelt Papers, FDRL.

53. Olin Dows, *Franklin Roosevelt at Hyde Park* (New York: American Artists Group, Inc., 1949), p. 97f.

54. Rhoads, "Artistic Patronage of Franklin D. Roosevelt," p. 17.

55. Henry T. Hackett, "The Hyde Park Patent," *Dutchess County Historical Society Year Book* 24 (1939): 75–90, p. 87f.

56. A caption in Margaret Logan Marquez, *Hyde Park on the Hudson,* (Dover, N.H.: Arcadia Publishing, 1996) mentions a 1791 map marked with two schoolhouses which, by tradition, were for children of slaves and for white children, p. 88.

57. William A. McVickar, D.D., *The Life of the Reverend John McVickar, S.T.D.* (New York: Hurd and Houghton, 1872), p. 30.

58. "Roosevelt Calls Our Free Schools a Bar to Tyranny," New York Times, October 6, 1940, p. 1.

59. "Informal Remarks of the President, Rhinebeck, New York, November 4, 1940," FDRL.

60. Rhoads, "Roosevelt and Dutch Colonial Architecture," p. 446; and Rhoads, "Artistic Patronage of Franklin D. Roosevelt," p. 16.

61. Rhoads, "Roosevelt and Dutch Colonial Architecture," p. 446f.

62. Katherine Stanley-Brown, unpublished journal.

63. *Closest Companion. The Unknown Story of the Intimate Friendship between Franklin Roosevelt and Margaret Suckley*, edited and annotated by Geoffrey C. Ward (Boston: Houghton Mifflin Company, 1995).

64. Ibid, p. 108. Letter dated November 4, 1937.

65. Ibid, p. 107.

66. Olin Dows, William Seabrook, and Chanler A. Chapman, *Murals in the Rhinebeck Post Office with Maps, a Description of the Murals and Notes on the Town* (Rhinebeck, N.Y.: Civic Club of Rhinebeck, 1940).

67. Rhoads, "Artistic Patronage of Franklin D. Roosevelt," p. 17.

68. Rhoads, "Olin Dows," p. 431 and n. 19. The quote is from the *Rhinebeck Gazette*, May 12, 1939.

69. "Text of Roosevelt Speech at the Dedication of the Rhinebeck Post Office Yesterday Afternoon," *Poughkeepsie Eagle-News*, May 2, 1939, p. 9.

70. Helen Wilkinson Reynolds, "President Roosevelt's First Speech Over the Radio," *Dutchess County Historical Society Year Book* 18 (1933): 34–36.

71. Rhoads, "Roosevelt and Dutch Colonial Architecture," p. 452.

72. National Archives, Record Group No. 121, Box 74, Entry 133, copy in Owen Gilleran, *The History of the Building of the Ellenville Post Office* (1998). This valuable compilation of archival materials was assembled by the son of the former Ellenville postmaster, James G. Gilleran.

73. FDR to Frank R. Wilson, May 10, 1939, *Personal Letters*, IV, 881, cited in Rhoads, "Roosevelt and Dutch Colonial Architecture," p. 453, n. 50.

74. Letter to Mr. Tuthill McDowell, town chairman, Ellenville, New York, May 19, 1939, signed Franklin D. Roosevelt. Copy to RSB. Gilleran, ed., *History of the Ellenville Post Office*.

75. A former Ellenville postmaster, Bill Tochterman, noted in a conversation on 27 April 2001, that the paneling in the lobby was said to have been modeled after paneling in the Hardenberg House. A 1938 photograph of a detail of the facade in the Ellenville

Museum with similar twelve-over-twelve sash windows and a narrow doorway strengthens the idea of this historic house as a partial model.

76. Katharine T. Terwilliger, *Wawarsing. Where the Streams Wind. Historical Glimpses of the Town* (Ellenville, N.Y.: The Rondout Valley Publishing Company, Inc., 1977), p. 249. The bell also was rung when President Lyndon B. Johnson made an official visit to Ellenville.

77. Letters dated January 23, and January 29, 1941, Gilleran, ed., *History of the Building*.

78. Ibid, Letter dated January 21, 1941. Gilleran has collected a good deal of correspondence between Bouché and Edward Rowan of the Section of Fine Arts and others which will be drawn upon here.

79. Marlene Park and Gerald E. Markowitz, *Democratic Vistas. Post Office and Public Art in the New Deal* (Philadelphia: Temple University Press, 1984), p. 14.

80. I would like to thank Mike McAffee, Curator of History and Uniforms, West Point Museum, for giving an expert opinion about this uniform and its source.

81. "Address of Henry Morgenthau, Jr., Secretary of the Treasury, at the laying of the cornerstone of the new Post Office at Poughkeepsie, N.Y., Wednesday, October 13, 1937," Morgenthau Diary, v. 92, pp. 58–61, FDRL.

82. The information about the Newburgh Peace stamp noted in the text comes from Brian C. Baur, *Franklin D. Roosevelt and the Stamps of the United States 1933–1945* (Sidney, Ohio: Linn's Stamp News, Amos Press, Inc., 1993), pp. 1–5, 167.

83. Roosevelt mentioned the connection in an election-eve stopover in 1940, "Informal Remarks. . .Newburgh, N.Y.," FDRL.

Acknowledgments

Mᴄⁱ INDEBTEDNESS to the work of the definitive scholar on FDR and architecture, William Rhoads, can be seen throughout the book. What is not apparent is Prof. Rhoads's personal encouragement for me to explore the topic further, saying there is always more to be discovered. Special thanks also to Cynthia Koch, director of the Franklin D. Roosevelt Library, and to John Sears, former director of the Franklin and Eleanor Roosevelt Institute, both of whom supported the idea of the book almost from the start.

I am indebted to several libraries for their resources and the helpful assistance of their staffs. First and foremost is the Franklin D. Roosevelt Library in Hyde Park. My thanks to the staff for their willingness to shepherd me through their remarkable collections step by step, and to Mark Renovich for securing photographs for the book with unfailing good cheer. Thanks to the Robert W. Woodruff Library, Emory University, where the research began. Once relocated in Poughkeepsie, I was able to utilize the Vassar College Library, Adriance Memorial Library; Howland Library, and the Ellenville Public Library and Museum, for which I am most grateful.

Special thanks to Katherine Stanley-Brown Abbott, who shared her knowledge of her architect father along with his publications, and to Katherine Worthington Taylor, who was similarly helpful in regard to her artist grandfather, Charles Rosen.

Other individuals and institutions also deserve my thanks. These include Joann Potter, registrar/collections manager, and the Frances Lehman Loeb Art Center, Vassar College; Robert Murphy and the Beacon Historical Society; Duane and Linda Watson and Linda Bouchey, Wilderstein Preservation; Kay Verrilli, The Museum of Rhinebeck History; Barbara

THE STAMP OF FDR

Sweet and Margaret Marquez, the Town of Hyde Park Historical Society. Linda Freaney, director of the Woodstock Artists Association, gave generous assistance more than once, as did Woodstock resident Polly Kline. Architectural historian Holly Wahlberg shared both her researches and her valuable insights over time.

The gracious reception of the postmasters, and their willingness to talk about their building and its history, added a special dimension to the project. So did the oral history gleaned from residents in each community connected with the post offices, past and present.

I am indebted to Hudson River Heritage for both personal and professional support. My thanks especially to the executive director, Kate Kerin, and to board members, Mike Gladstone and Mimi Dunne.

Sincere thanks to Furthermore, the publication program of the J. M. Kaplan Fund, for a publication grant. And resounding thanks to Ted Spiegel, color photographer, and Wray Rominger, co-publisher of Purple Mountain Press Ltd., who put their own professional stamps on the book, thereby enhancing its quality no end.

Index

Also available from Purple Mountain Press:
The Hudson Valley Dutch and Their Houses
by Harrison Meeske

For the first time since the 1930s there is a new book about the earliest European settlers in the Hudson Valley and the building styles they brought with them and modified in their new home.

412 pages, illustrated, 6 x 9, bibliography, index